A DEFENSE OF THE TRINITY

(Doctrinal, Practical, and Historical)

Index

Introduction

The Biblical doctrine of the Trinity has been hotly contested for many years. The early church battled various heresies that denied the Trinity in differing ways. Although the Council of Nicaea in AD325 codified the doctrine of the Trinity, it by no means settled the issue, as it continues to be debated and disputed today.

From the very beginning of my ministry, I have been very interested in the doctrine of the Trinity and have invested hundreds of hours in studying it. While we can only receive the doctrine by faith in the Divine revelation we call Scripture, we can certainly recognize the reality and truthfulness of the doctrine. As I have studied, I have learned more and more the value of this doctrine and the stability it gives to the believer as well as how it leads us to worship.

It will be my aim to demonstrate in this defense of the doctrine of the Trinity the following: the Trinity is necessary and cannot be otherwise, the Bible teaches One God in three Persons, this doctrine affects our salvation, sanctification, and worship, and rejecting the Trinity is a dangerous and damnable heresy. Finally, I demonstrate from the pages of history that the Trinitarian faith is the faith of the earliest Christians.

It is my desire and prayer this book will profit those who read it by leading each one to worship more deeply as well as helping in the defense of the faith.

A Doctrinal Defense of The Trinity

God The Necessary Being

Is God real? This is among the most important of all questions asked. It is also the one that we must settle before we begin a long series on Christian doctrine. After all, Christian doctrine is of no use if there is no God.

How does one go about proving the existence of God? He cannot be seen with the eye. God cannot be measured with a scale or a ruler. God cannot be found through scientific experimentation. Christians, however, are convinced that the Trinitarian God of the Bible is real. How can we ever establish His existence as a matter of fact?

As we begin with the existence of God, we must go to one of the most basic and most important issues of life: **meaning**[1]. Once we begin to speak of meaning, different ideas arise. Some believe there is no meaning. Ironically enough, they expect us to understand the meaning of their words as they speak to us. Others say that all is **relative**[2], and meaning changes. Yet others speak of **absolutes**[3], and declare that meaning is neither related to, nor dependent upon, anything; but meaning exists independently.

---

[1] Meaning is what is meant by a word, concept, or action. It also deals with the worthwhile nature and purpose of something.

[2] That which is relative is dependent upon something else.

[3] An absolute is a value or principle that is universally valid or able to be viewed without relating it to other things.

All of us live as if there is meaning, and as if there are absolutes. When we get a paycheck, and when we make our deposits in the bank, we are definitely convinced math has meaning, and that the principles of addition and subtraction are absolute. We have no desire for anyone to deal with our money (And we feel the same about the rest of our lives, too.) as if mathematical principles are relative. Furthermore, we live with the understanding that time is an absolute. We all mark time in hours, minutes, and seconds. Though the language may be different from one nation to the next, we all understand time has meaning, and that there are twenty-four hours in a day. If we did not do so, all would be chaotic.

This belief in absolutes is especially relevant when it comes to the things we know and consider to be true. Truth cannot be relative. By nature, that which is true cannot be false at the same time. This is called the law of non-contradiction, and it tells us that something cannot be A and Non-A simultaneously.

For us to have absolutes, we must have an absolute **standard**[4]. We measure our days by the rotation of the earth. We measure our years by the orbit of Earth around the sun. This means that we recognize our watches and our calendars must be reset at times, because a solar year is a bit longer than our calendar year is. Thus, we have a leap year every four years. Why? Because we are measuring our time by the standard of the time it takes the earth to make a complete revolution around the sun.

---

[4] A standard is that by which all else is measured.

Now, the rotation and orbit of the earth are not necessarily absolute. They are subject to change. When it comes to truth, we need an absolute standard, because we speak of truth versus falsehood; and we recognize that truth is absolute. But where does truth get its truthfulness? What is the standard of truth? What is the source of truth? For the answer to these questions, we must turn to the Scriptures, and we shall see that the Christian's Bible gives him the only logically coherent view of truth, knowledge, and the world.

"*IN the beginning God created the heaven and the earth.*"
(Genesis 1:1)

There must be a source of all things. There must be a cause of all things. There cannot exist an effect without there first being a cause. The world did not come into being on its own power. There must be a beginning cause that is uncaused. [5] Christians understand that this uncaused cause is the Creator, the God who is presented to us in the Bible.

Creation testifies to us that God exists. The Psalmist tells us, "*The heavens declare the glory of God; And the*

[5] To say there is no God is to hold that the world exists on its own as its own creator, or that there is an infinite series of causes that brought the world into existence. Neither of these ideas are actual solutions to the question of origins. The first presents the idea of a self-caused cause, which is impossible and illogical. The latter posits an infinite regress, which is impossible, because there will of necessity be a cause that is the first of all causes.

firmament sheweth his handywork. Day unto day uttereth speech, And night unto night sheweth knowledge. There is no speech nor language, Where their voice is not heard." (Psalm 19:1–3) Wherever one goes there is testimony to the existence of God. The starry heaven and all that is in the sky above us tell us God is great, valuable, and beautiful. Their beauty, balance, and order tell us that were designed by a mighty, beautiful, and intelligent person.

Not only do the skies and heavens above us testify to the existence and presence of God, but all of Creation tells us He is here with us. "*For the wrath of God is revealed from heaven against all ungodliness and unrighteousness of men, who hold the truth in unrighteousness; because that which may be known of God is manifest in them; for God hath shewed it unto them. For the invisible things of him from the creation of the world are clearly seen, being understood by the things that are made, even his eternal power and Godhead; so that they are without excuse:*" (Romans 1:18–20) Creation testifies to us that God exists, because we know there must be a cause for all things, and that cause must be beautiful (i.e. glorious), eternal (timeless), and forever powerful. After all, matter, beauty, and time could not exist except a beautiful, all powerful, and intelligent person existed outside of time and made it all.

There is also a seasonal cycle that testifies to God's personal existence. The succession of the four seasons provides us with that which is necessary to the production of the food that sustains us. This order of events speaks to us of the fact that an orderly and intelligent person made the Earth to do these things. Paul preached, telling some idol worshipers, "*We also are men of like passions with you, and preach unto you that ye should turn from these vanities unto the living God, which made heaven, and earth, and the sea, and all things that are therein: who in times past suffered all nations to walk in their own ways. Nevertheless he left not himself without witness, in that he did good, and gave us rain from heaven, and fruitful seasons, filling our hearts with food and gladness.*" (Acts 14:15–17) This Creator must be a person, because He made persons, and He acts in a personal manner by showing kindness to His creatures: kindness that gives us joy.

If one were to believe the illogical theory that everything came into being by nothing, out of nothing, by random and meaningless processes, there would be no reason for them to think there was any meaning to anything. After all, there would be no intelligent creator and ruler who had the ability and authority to give meaning. On the other hand, those of us who understand God created all things believe and know He has a purpose for all things and gives all things meaning.

As we saw above in Romans 1:18-20 God has shown Himself to us in Creation. This means the created order speaks to us primarily of God. In fact, Genesis 1:1 opens us the Bible telling us about God. He reveals Himself to His creatures by instructing them and giving them purpose. He also reveals Himself to us in the Scriptures. This is why the Bible begins by telling us all started with God: He is revealing Himself to us so we will know Him and His will and purpose for us.

God has revealed Himself to us, and Creation is first and foremost about God and His purposes. When we look around us and think about the world, we must think of it as

God's world, filled with God's meaning, and made for God's purposes.

Furthermore, this world has no other standard of truth than God. God is one (Deuteronomy 6:4-5), and He alone is the arbiter and source of knowledge and truth (Deuteronomy 32:4;1Samuel 2:3; John 14:6[6];2Corinthians 1:18;1John 2:27). Why is He the standard? Because He is the only absolute, eternal, unchanging God. He also is our Creator. "If the Christian position with respect to creation, that is, with respect to the idea of the origin of both the subject and the object of human knowledge is true, there is and must be objective knowledge. In that case the world of objects was made in order that the subject of knowledge, namely man, should interpret it under God. Without the interpretation of the universe by man to the glory of God the whole world would be meaningless. The subject and object are therefore adapted to one another. On the other hand, if the Christian theory of creation by God is not true then we hold that there cannot be objective knowledge of

---

6 It is interesting to note the bearing that this has upon the discussion of the Genesis Creation Account, because John 14:6 builds upon John 1:1-4 and Jesus' being the creator. Cornelius Van Til said regarding this, "If the Christian position with respect to creation, that is, with respect to the idea of the origin of both the subject and the object of human knowledge is true, there is and must be objective knowledge. In that case the world of objects was made in order that the subject of knowledge, namely man, should interpret it under God. Without the interpretation of the universe by man to the glory of God the whole world would be meaningless. The subject and object are therefore adapted to one another. On the other hand if the Christian theory of creation by God is not true then we hold that there cannot be objective knowledge of anything. In that case all things in this universe are unrelated and cannot be in fruitful contact with one another. This we believe to be the simple alternative on the question of the objectivity of knowledge as far as the things of this universe are concerned."

Cornelius Van Til, The Defense Of The Faith, P&R, Philadelphia, PA, pg 43

anything. In that case all things in this universe are unrelated and cannot be in fruitful contact with one another. This we believe to be the simple alternative on the question of the objectivity of knowledge as far as the things of this universe are concerned."7 There is simply no other way that there can be coherence and rationality. Either God the Creator is the sole and absolute standard and authority, with all things relating to Him and subordinate to Him, or there is no knowledge, truth, or **rationality**[8].

If there can be no knowledge or truth apart from God, then God is a **necessary**[9] being. In other words, God must exist, because there is no logical way for there to be no God. If one denies God, he must also deny truth and meaning. If he denies truth and meaning, all is random, chaotic, and relative. No one lives as if that were true, however. We all live as if there is meaning and truth in life. To speak of meaning and truth is to acknowledge there is a standard of meaning and truth, and this invariably brings us back to the necessity of God's existence.

Finally, we should take notice of the fact that we have not only seen the logical need for God, but we have seen that the Bible presents to us the God who is needed. The Bible provides us the framework for rational thought, as it presents to us God as the Creator who is the source and standard of all knowledge and truth. This means, not only have we established a good case for the existence of God, but we have also found good reason to believe the Bible. Without the Bible, we have

7 Cornelius Van Til, The Defense Of The Faith, P&R, Philadelphia, PA, pg 43

8 Rationality is that which accords with reason or logic.

9 That which is necessary is inevitable. It cannot be otherwise.

no means by which we can establish that there is absolute truth and meaning.

The One True God Is the Triune God of Christianity

"*In the beginning God created the heaven and the earth. And the earth was without form, and void; and darkness was upon the face of the deep. And the Spirit of God moved upon the face of the waters. And God said, Let there be light: and there was light.*" (Genesis 1:1–3)

The Triune God

This text, in the context of the totality of Scripture, gives to us an understanding of God as a plurality in unity, as it speaks to us of God creating and the Spirit being present. We must specifically, when speaking of the God of the Bible, speak of God as a Tri-unity, or Trinity. The one God is three persons in perfect unity of being, essence, and agreement. We see this by considering the fact that the Son is as much Creator-God as the Father (See John 1:1-4,14 and Hebrews 1:1-3), and by understanding that the Spirit of God is equally Divine (Job 33:4, Acts 5:1-5 and Romans 8:9-10). These three persons, Father, Son, and Spirit, are the One God.

Why Is the Triune God Necessary?

Why would we say the Triune God of Scripture is necessary to knowledge?

First, truth is expected to be a unity. We expect that which is true in one field of study to agree with what is true in any other field of study in whatever fashion those fields of truth intersect. For example, we would expect that mathematical truth would be the same whether it was applied to governments or to a building contractor's business. We would not expect the realities of mathematics to change simply because of the field in which math was applied changed. We expect truth to be true wherever truth appears.

What this means is, we expect there to be unity in plurality. While there are many fields of knowledge, we expect the truth to be united across the plurality of fields. There is one body of truth, though many fields of knowledge; and the truths found in every field of knowledge agree, as truth is an unity.

The problem is, we must then find a source and standard for truth and knowledge that can provide unity in plurality.

Pantheism cannot provide this unity in plurality. If all is god, then there is actually more of a monad than a plurality. Not only so, but all is subsumed into god leaving us with obscurity. There would be no true revelation, because all is god and there would be nothing distinct from the god to receive knowledge. In fact, we would be unable to even know what to call this god. This would cause everyone and everything to be a standard of truth in and of itself/ourselves. This would leave us with relativism, because we would be unable to point anywhere to a united standard of truth that addresses the problem of plurality in unity.

If God were totally one in the sense that Allah, the god of the Muslims, is one, then we would again have an unknowable standard. The god would then be so utterly other than the world and humanity as to be unapproachable and unknowable. There would be no way to have a divine revelation to give us truth and knowledge. Neither would we have a standard by which to know truth. We would be left in the dark. The same can be said about the god of Modalism and

Absolute Oneness, which declares the Father, Son, and Holy Spirit are not only one god but one person.

What, then, is the answer to our dilemma? The Triune God of Scripture is the answer. He alone meets our need for a single, sovereign, intelligent Creator God who is the source of all knowledge and truth. Apart from the Trinity there can be neither truth nor knowledge.

The Bible, as the source of our knowledge of this Triune God, is our only ground of rational thought. It is in the Christian Scriptures that we find that God is:

1. Our Creator (Genesis 1:1-3;Jeremiah 32:17;Hebrews 1:1-3;11:3).
2. The God of knowledge and truth who judges us (Deuteronomy 32:4;1Samuel 2:3).
3. The God who is one God, yet three persons (Genesis 1:1-3,26-28;Psalm 110:1-7;John 1:1-4,14;3:16-17;5:17-21;Hebrews 1:1-3).
4. The God who makes Himself known to His creatures (Genesis 1:1-31;2:1-25;Psalm 19:1-11;Isaiah 40:1-8;John 1:18;Hebrews 1:1-3;Revelation 1:1-8;22:1-6,16-21).

We then conclude the Trinity is necessary because there would be no being, knowledge, or reason apart from the Triune God of Scripture. Thus, we conclude the Trinity is true and necessary.

The Necessity of The Trinity as Seen in God's Character

The cornerstone of Biblical doctrine and Christianity is the doctrine of God. Who is God? What is His nature? How does He manifest Himself to us, and how does He work? While I shall make no attempt to answer all these questions, it is imperative we learn the fundamental truth of the Trinity. The doctrine of the Trinity is not arrived at by philosophical searching; it is a doctrine known only by revelation. While the eternal power and deity of God is manifest in creation, the Trinity is only shown to us in the revealed Word of God, the Scriptures.

One thing that is necessary to state is the fact the Trinity does not teach that there are three gods. On the contrary, the term Trinity speaks of three in unity, or tri-unity. When we speak of the Trinity, we mean three in one. The Scriptures bear witness of this fact saying, *"For there are three that bear record in heaven, the Father, the Word, and the Holy Ghost: and these three are one." (1 John 5:7)* When the Scriptures tell us the Father, the Word, and the Holy Ghost are one they are telling us hey exist as one. The very being of God is one. The three who are in God exist as one. There is only one God who truly exists, but there are three persons in this being we call God. God's Word attests to the fact of the solitary existence of God in a plurality of persons. *"but to us there is but one God, the Father, of whom are all things, and we in him; and one Lord Jesus Christ, by whom are all things, and we by him." (1 Corinthians 8:6)* Paul is telling us there is only one God, as opposed to the belief in many gods that idolaters hold. He states there is only one God, and names two of the persons who are God: the Father, and the Lord Jesus Christ. While he names *two* persons, he calls the two persons the *one* God!

As we consider this subject, the question should be asked, "why speak of the *necessity* of the Trinity?" Webster's 1828 Dictionary defines necessity thusly: "That which must be and cannot be otherwise." When we speak of the Trinity being necessary, we mean God's nature is such that He must be a plurality of persons who are of one essence. The Bible reveals to us that this God is a Tri-unity of persons, hence the Trinity.

The Glory of God Makes the Trinity Necessary

God is eternally glorious. God's glory is His nature and character. He shines forth in splendor, beauty, and might. This glorious nature of God makes the Trinity a necessity.

The first attribute of God's glory we will consider is the name of God. When we speak of God's name, we speak of the reputation and fame of God as well as the appellation by which He is called. God told Moses that His name was an eternal name/fame. *"And Moses said unto God, Behold, when I come unto the children of Israel, and shall say unto them, The God of your fathers hath sent me unto you; and they shall say to me, What is his name? what shall I say unto them? And God said unto Moses, I AM THAT I AM: and he said, Thus shalt thou say unto the children of Israel, I AM hath sent me unto you. And God said moreover unto Moses, Thus shalt thou say unto the children of Israel, The LORD God of your fathers, the God of Abraham, the God of Isaac, and the God of Jacob, hath sent me unto you: this is my name for ever, and this is my memorial unto all generations." (Exodus 3:13–15)*

If God's fame and glory are eternal, there must have been a plurality of persons present to see and enjoy this fame. True fame does not rest in one's mind alone. The fame and glory of God were expressed and enjoyed in eternity before even the angels were created. God enjoyed His glory as He beheld His Son (See Prov 8:30;John 17:5,24).

God's glory is also seen in His mercy and truth. *"Not unto us, O LORD, not unto us, But unto thy name give glory, For thy mercy, and for thy truth's sake." (Psalm 115:1)* God is eternally merciful and true. He has always been this way. These are personal attributes. In other words, mercy and truth are shared with other persons. For God to be eternally merciful and true makes it necessary for there to have always been other persons to whom He expressed mercy and truth. (Note: Mercy here does not primarily speak of God's compassion to those who face hardship and judgment but is the loving-kindness of God which He expresses to other persons and has expressed forever to the other persons of the Godhead.) From this we see God is a plurality of persons.

Love Makes the Trinity Necessary

The Bible tells us God is love (See 1 Jn 4:8). The love of God is such that, if God ceased to love at all He would no longer be God. God does not only love but *is* love. When we consider the fact that God is eternal (Ps 90:1,2; Rom 1:20), God has always been love and has always loved. For God to have always loved, there must be one who was there to be loved before the world was made. That one who was present and loved before the world was created must also be eternal. This being so, this one would be equal to God. This means there would be more than one person in the essence of God.

As we read the Bible, we find that this one who is loved is none other than the Son of God, who is also called the Word. "*IN the beginning was the Word, and the Word was with God, and the Word was God. The same was in the beginning with*

God. All things were made by him; and without him was not any thing made that was made." (John 1:1–3) "And the Word was made flesh, and dwelt among us, (and we beheld his glory, the glory as of the only begotten of the Father,) full of grace and truth." (John 1:14) The reader will recall the Word being spoken of as being one with the Father and the Holy Ghost. Now we find the Word was present in the creation and is God. How is this so? Perhaps it would be well to try to describe it in this manner: As person looks at life, they will find themselves thinking about particular moments in life. As these moments are contemplated, one finds that many emotions come to them as though they are reliving the moment. Should one be able to have a perfect thought of every moment of his life, that thought would then become a complete replica of that person. When God is considered as contemplating His eternal greatness and having a perfect thought of Himself, that thought is spoken of as the Word (logos), because it would be both a perfect representation of His thought and (words being expressions of thoughts) would be an eternal person equal to the Father and of the same essence. We know Jesus is the Word of God who is the expression of the nature, heart, character and will of God in eternity and in this world (See John 1:1-4; Heb 1:1-3). The Word is also the Son of God, because God is spoken of as the Father of whom are all things. He would also be the Son because He is of the same nature as the Father. He is not created but is eternally generated and eternally co-equal with the Father. He has no beginning nor end, because God has always had the perfect thought of Himself.

Jesus spoke of this great love that exists between Him and the Father. *"Father, I will that they also, whom thou hast given me, be with me where I am; that they may behold my glory, which thou hast given me: for thou lovedst me before the foundation of the world." (John 17:24) In* fact, this love between the Father and the Son is so intense it is another person. That person is the Holy Spirit. Have you ever been around a group of people where, although there are many individual persons, there is a group spirit? We call it esprit de corps. The spirit of the body. It seems the group of people has a personality in itself. So it is in the Godhead. The Father loves the Son and the Son loves the Father. This eternal love is so great it has a personality and is a person. Jesus' own words bear witness to this fact. *"And I have declared unto them thy name, and will declare it: that the love wherewith thou hast loved me may be in them, and I in them." (John 17:26)* Notice that Jesus spoke of the love of the Father and Himself dwelling in us. Who is it that dwells in us? Paul says it is Christ (Col 1:27) We find also that *"the love of God is shed abroad in our hearts by the Holy Ghost which is given unto us." (Romans 5:5)* The Spirit of God dwells within us spreading God's love in our hearts. We are also told, *"Now if any man have not the Spirit of Christ, he is none of his." (Romans 8:9)* It is evident that the love which exists in the Godhead is the one we call the third person of the Godhead, the Holy Spirit.

This, I believe, is the Biblical doctrine of the Holy Trinity. This doctrine is a revealed doctrine. We do not by searching find God out. This is not seen in Creation, nor inherently understood. It is not understood at all. We simply embrace this truth because God has revealed it to us. This truth demonstrates to us that our God is truly transcendent. Let us, therefore, worship Him in all His Tri-une glory. "*Holy, holy, holy, is the LORD of hosts: The whole earth is full of his glory." (Isaiah 6:3) "The grace of the Lord Jesus Christ, and the love of God, and the communion of the Holy Ghost, be with you all. Amen." (2 Corinthians 13:14)* [10]

---

[10] I am greatly indebted to Jonathan Edwards' "Unpublished Essay on The Trinity" as a resource for this chapter. https://ccel.org/ccel/edwards/trinity/files/trinity.html (Accessed May 16, 2025)

The Biblical Doctrine of The Trinity

The Creation Account and The Implied Trinity

"In the beginning God created the heaven and the earth. And the earth was without form, and void; and darkness was upon the face of the deep. And the Spirit of God moved upon the face of the waters." (Gen 1:1-2) "And God said, Let us make man in our image, after our likeness: and let them have dominion over the fish of the sea, and over the fowl of the air, and over the cattle, and over all the earth, and over every creeping thing that creepeth upon the earth. So God created man in his own image, in the image of God created he him; male and female created he them." (Gen 1:26-27)

The Genre of The Genesis Account of Creation

At the outset, let it be known that this writer understands there are those who will refuse to accept the fact of the Trinity being present in the above verses. They may contend the account of creation as seen in Genesis chapters one and two is not a literal, historical narrative, but rather a poetic narrative that does not yield itself to a literal reading and interpretation. Is this truly so?

The form of the creation account is historic. It gives a chronological procession of events. We are told of how the creation took place from day to day. The days are literal twenty-four-hour days, as we can see from Moses: *"In six days the LORD made heaven and earth, the sea, and all that in them is, and rested the seventh day: wherefore the LORD blessed the sabbath day, and hallowed it." (Ex 20:11)* This again points us to the Genesis account being a literal, historical record of the creation. Furthermore, Jesus taught the Genesis account of creation to be a literal, historical record (See Matt 12:8;19:3-6), the writer of Hebrews understood it to be the same (See Heb

4:4;11:3), the Psalmist understood the same (Ps 33:6-11;136:1-9), as did Solomon (Prov 3:19,20), and the list could surely be continued. Of those who choose to call the Genesis creation account a sort of poem a question must be asked: would not some of the prophets or apostles, or even (I might say especially) Jesus have learned that this was not literal history, but only a poetic statement of God's creating the world and informed us of this fact? A view that considers the Genesis account of creation to be anything other than literal history calls into question the knowledge, character, and integrity of Jesus, who taught it to be literally true. This writer is content to believe this account was given to us that we might know the literal, historical truth about the creation of the world and the God who created it.

(Note: Though this writer affords no more authority to the Early Church Fathers than he does to elders whom he is to respect today, it is interesting to note that Augustine believed the Genesis account of creation to be historical, though he seemed at times confused in his interpretation of it. "What then is this introduction? 'In the beginning God made the heaven and the earth, and the earth was invisible, and unformed? and darkness was upon the face of the abyss.' Do these words seem to some of you incapable of affording consolation under distress? Is it not an historical narrative, and an instruction about the creation?"

Schaff, P. (2000). *The Nicene Fathers* (electronic ed.). Garland, TX: Galaxie Software.

The Name of God in The Creation Account

Biblical languages are rich. We can learn much from them. With the resources available today one can learn much without having learned the original languages (Though the writer recommends one attempting to gain at least a rudimentary understanding of the original languages of Scripture.). The Hebrew name for God in Genesis 1:1 is *Elohim*. Let us learn to what *Elohim* points us.

"That there is such a plurality of persons, will appear more clearly, from the plural names and epithets of God. His great and incommunicable name Jehovah, is always in the singular number, and is never used plurally; the reason of which is, because it is expressive of his essence, which is but one; it is the same with " I AM that I AM "; but the first name of God we meet with in scripture, and that in the first verse of it, is plural; "In the beginning God (Elohim) created the heaven and the earth", (Gen. 1:1) and therefore must design more than one, at least two, and yet not precisely two, or two only; then it would have been dual; but it is plural; and, as the Jews themselves say, cannot design fewer than three. Now Moses might have made use of other names of God, in his account of the creation; as his name Jehovah, by which he made himself known to him, and to the people of Israel; or Eloah, the singular of Elohim, which is used by him, (Deut. 32:15, 16) and in the book of Job frequently; so that it was not want of singular names of God, nor the barrenness of the Hebrew language, which obliged him to use a plural word; it was no doubt of choice, and with design; and which will be more evident when it is observed, that one end of the writings of Moses is to extirpate the polytheism of the heathens, and to prevent the people of Israel from going into it; and therefore it may seem strange, that he should begin his history with a plural name of God; he must have some design in it, which could not be to inculcate a plurality of gods, for that would be directly contrary to what he had in view in writing, and to what he asserts, (Deut. 6:4). "Hear, O Israel, the Lord our God is one Lord": nor a plurality of mere names and characters, to which creative powers cannot be ascribed; but a plurality of persons, for so the words may be rendered, distributively, according to the idiom of the Hebrew language; "In the beginning everyone, or each of the divine persons, created the heaven and the earth". And then the historian goes on to make mention of them; who, besides the Father, included in this name, are the Spirit of God, that moved upon the face of the waters, and the word of God, (Gen. 1:2) which said, "Let there be light, and there was light"; and which spoke that, and all things, out of nothing; see (John 1:1-3)."[11]

In Genesis 1:1, the original word *Elohim,* "God," is certainly the plural form of *El*, or *Eloah,* and has long been supposed, by the most eminently learned and pious men, to imply a plurality of persons in the divine nature. As this plurality appears in so many parts of the sacred writings to be confined to three persons, hence the doctrine of the TRINITY, which has formed a part of the creed of all those who have been deemed sound in the faith, from the earliest ages of Christianity. Nor are the Christians singular in receiving this doctrine, and in deriving it from the first words of divine revelation. An eminent Jewish rabbin, Simeon ben Joachi, has these remarkable words: "Come and see the mystery of the

---

[11] John Gill. *A BODY OF DOCTRINAL DIVINITY* (179). Formatted for use with Logos Bible Software by Joseph Kreifels.

word *Elohim;* there are three degrees, and each degree by itself alone, and yet, notwithstanding, they are all one, and joined together in one, and are not divided from each other."[12] In the ever blessed Trinity, from the infinite and indivisible unity of the persons, there can be but one will, one purpose, and one infinite and uncontrollable energy.

---

[12] Clarke, A. (1999). *Christian Theology* (electronic ed.). Albany, OR: Ages Software.

Jesus Our Divine Creator

As we consider the Trinity as implied and seen in the Creation, we must recognize that the leading person in the Creation was God the Father. *"God, who at sundry times and in divers manners spake in time past unto the fathers by the prophets, Hath in these last days spoken unto us by his Son, whom he hath appointed heir of all things, by whom also he made the worlds; Who being the brightness of his glory, and the express image of his person, and upholding all things by the word of his power, when he had by himself purged our sins, sat down on the right hand of the Majesty on high; Being made so much better than the angels, as he hath by inheritance obtained a more excellent name than they." (Heb 1:1-4)* God the Father took the lead in the Creation but, when He created, He did so by the Son. Notice how the Psalmist alludes to this: *"By the word of the LORD were the heavens made; and all the host of them by the breath of his mouth." (Ps 33:6)* Today we understand the Psalmist was not only saying creation was by Divine fiat but was also alluding to the Father creating the worlds by Christ. "We may truly and certainly infer from this passage, that the world was framed by God's Eternal Word, his only begotten Son."[13]

---

[13] Calvin, J. (2000). *Calvin's Commentaries* (electronic ed.). electronic ed. (Ps 33:6). Garland, TX: Galaxie Software.

The New Testament gives us ample testimony to the fact of the deity of Christ, using the creative work of God to do so. John opens his account of Christ by saying, *"In the beginning was the Word, and the Word was with God, and the Word was God. The same was in the beginning with God. All things were made by him; and without him was not any thing made that was made. In him was life; and the life was the light of men." (Jn 1:1-4)* Even if we were to grant the contention of the Russellites (which we do not) that the translation should be "the Word was *a* god," we must still conclude that the Word in this passage is more than one god among many. Why? We must come to this conclusion because the Word is the very self-expression of God; the very mind, heart, and character of God; the eternal and perfect understanding that the Father has of Himself. When God is considered as contemplating His eternal greatness and having a perfect thought of Himself, that thought is spoken of as the Word (logos), because it would be both a perfect representation of His thought and (words being expressions of thoughts) would be an eternal person equal to the Father and of the same essence. We know Jesus is the Word of God who is the expression of the nature, heart, character and will of God in eternity and in this world. Thus, it is that the Son is spoken of as being eternally begotten of the Father. Never has there been a time that the Father has not had this perfect awareness of His eternal self, and so there has never been a time the Son/Word was not.

The Word is spoken of as being with God in the beginning. That is, the Word was before the creation. This means the Word is eternal in nature. Immortality is the unique attribute of God (1Tim 6:16). He alone has immortality. If the Word was with God before the creation of the worlds, then He is necessarily immortal, and thus necessarily God. Not only so, but, referring back to the great I AM of Exodus (See Ex 3:13-15), John tells us that not only is the Word the immortal God and Creator, but He is this I AM; the one who has an underived existence. In Him, the Word, was life. The Word, God, the Creator is the source of all life. In other words, the Word is the JEHOVAH of the Old Testament, the God of Israel. Then we read, *"the Word was made flesh, and dwelt among us, (and we beheld his glory, the glory as of the only begotten of the Father,) full of grace and truth." (Jn 1:14) This* confirms to us that the writer is indeed telling us of Jesus, and that Jesus is the eternal Son of God.

The deity of Christ in relation to the creation is confirmed to us as we read the New Testament. Paul wrote to the Colossians and told them of Jesus: *"Who is the image of the invisible God, the firstborn of every creature: For by him were all things created, that are in heaven, and that are in earth, visible and invisible, whether they be thrones, or dominions, or principalities, or powers: all things were created by him, and for him: And he is before all things, and by him all things consist." (Col 1:15-17)* We again read, *"God, who at sundry times and in divers manners spake in time past unto the fathers by the prophets, Hath in these last days spoken unto us by his Son, whom he hath appointed heir of all things, by whom also he made the worlds; Who being the brightness of his glory, and the express image of his person, and upholding all things by the word of his power, when he had by himself purged our sins, sat down on the right hand of the Majesty on high." (Heb 1:1-3)* These two passages present to us the Son as being the Creator and the image of God. What is meant by the image of God? In the Colossian passage image speaks of the resemblance between God the Father and the Son. "In Col. 1:15 Christ is described as the εἰκὼν τοῦ θεοῦ τοῦ ἀοράτου. To modern logic this seems to be a contradiction, for how can there be an image of something which is invisible and without form? The peculiarity of the expression is related to that of the ancient concept, which does not limit image to a functional representation present to human sense but also thinks of it in terms of an emanation, of a revelation of the being with a substantial participation (μετοχή) in the object._ Image is not to be understood as a magnitude which is alien to the reality and present only in the consciousness. It has a share in the reality. Indeed, it is the reality. Thus, εἰκών does not imply a weakening or a feeble copy of something. It implies the illumination of its inner core and essence."[14] We see, then, that the

---

14 *Theological dictionary of the New Testament.* 1964-c1976. Vols. 5-9 edited by Gerhard Friedrich. Vol. 10 compiled by Ronald Pitkin. (G. Kittel, G. W.

Son's being the image of God means He is the perfect representation of the person and attributes of God and is therefore God. The Hebrews passage is a little different but speaks of the same reality that is presented by the Son being the image of God. The writer of Hebrews stated the Son is the express image of the person of God. The image in this sense gives us a picture of a stamp that leaves its exact impression upon the document that is stamped. Jesus is said to bear the exact imprint of the character of God. If He does so, then He is God, because one cannot be exactly like God without being God.

We then find the Son is the radiance of the splendor and glory of the Father. He simply shines forth the glorious character of the Father in every way possible. This is why John stated that the glory which was seen in Christ was the glory as of the only begotten of the Father. The glory radiating from Jesus is manifested as (See 1Tim 3:16) the Divine glory of the Father; yet it was the glory of the Son as well.

In both the Colossian and the Hebrew passage Jesus is spoken of as the Creator and sustainer of the worlds. Everything was created by Him [Nothing was created without Him (See Jn 1:3).], all things are sustained by Him, and all things were created for Him. For the average Bible reader, it is not difficult to

---

Bromiley & G. Friedrich, Ed.) (electronic ed.) (2:389). Grand Rapids, MI: Eerdmans.

understand there is no Creator beside God, and thus Jesus is God.

[Note: The Colossian and Johannine use of the word "begotten" in reference to the Son is used by some to insist that Jesus was the Son only by incarnation. This is impossible due to the fact the Son was the Son of God before He was incarnate (See Isa 9:6; Jn 3:16,17 where the Son is said to have been given and sent as opposed to being created or made.). The Scriptures obviously describe the Son of God as having existed before the Creation. Colossians 1:12-19 explicitly shows the Son of God is eternally the Son.]

Having considered that the worlds were made by the Son, we find new meaning when we read, *"Let all the earth fear the LORD: let all the inhabitants of the world stand in awe of him. For he spake, and it was done; he commanded, and it stood fast." (Ps 33:8-9)* God the Father spoke, and God the Son acted. God the Father and God the Son both created by means of Divine fiat.

The Spirit of God as Seen in The Creation

When we read the Genesis account of the creation of the heavens and the earth we read, *"In the beginning God created the heaven and the earth. And the earth was without form, and void; and darkness was upon the face of the deep. And the Spirit of God moved upon the face of the waters." (Gen 1:1-2)* It is readily seen that the Spirit of God was active in the creation of the worlds. Now we must determine who this Spirit of God is. Because God is the only Creator, we are convinced the Spirit is a divine person. Seeing there are those who do not readily take this for granted, let us search the Scriptures to see if this is so.

One thing leading us to understand the Holy Spirit is divine is the fact that He is spoken of as having the divine incommunicable attributes. That is, The Holy Spirit has attributes belonging only to God.

He is eternal as God is eternal. *"Lord, thou hast been our dwelling place in all generations. Before the mountains were brought forth, or ever thou hadst formed the earth and the world, even from everlasting to everlasting, thou art God." (Ps 90:1,2) "If the blood of bulls and of goats, and the ashes of an heifer sprinkling the unclean, sanctifieth to the purifying of the flesh: How much more shall the blood of Christ, who through the eternal Spirit offered himself without spot to God, purge your conscience from dead works to serve the living God?" (Heb 9:13,14)*

The Holy Spirit is also spoken of as being omniscient. All knowledge belongs to God and no one else. *"The word of God is quick, and powerful, and sharper than any twoedged sword, piercing even to the dividing asunder of soul and spirit, and of the joints and marrow, and is a discerner of the thoughts and intents of the heart. Neither is there any creature that is not manifest in his sight: but all things are naked and opened unto the eyes of him with whom we have to do." (Heb 4:12,13)* This attribute also belongs to the Spirit of

God. *"The Spirit searcheth all things, yea, the deep things of God." (1 Cor 2:10)*

The Spirit of God is also spoken of as being omnipresent, which is also a divine attribute. *"Am I a God at hand, saith the Lord, and not a God afar off? Can any hide himself in secret places that I shall not see him? saith the Lord. Do not I fill heaven and earth? saith the Lord." (Jer 23:23,24) "Whither shall I go from thy spirit? or whither shall I flee from thy presence? If I ascend up into heaven, thou art there: if I make my bed in hell, behold, thou art there. If I take the wings of the morning, and dwell in the uttermost parts of the sea; Even there shall thy hand lead me, and thy right hand shall hold me. If I say, Surely the darkness shall cover me; even the night shall be light about me. Yea, the darkness hideth not from thee; but the night shineth as the day: the darkness and the light are both alike to thee." (Ps 139:7-12)*

Finally, the Holy Spirit is spoken of as being omnipotent just as God is omnipotent. *"I heard as it were the voice of a great multitude, and as the voice of many waters, and as the voice of mighty thunderings, saying, Alleluia: for the Lord God omnipotent reigneth." (Rev 19:6) "The angel answered and said unto her, The Holy Ghost shall come upon thee, and the power of the Highest shall overshadow thee: therefore also that holy thing which shall be born of thee shall be called the Son of God. And, behold, thy cousin Elisabeth, she hath also conceived a son in her old age: and this is the sixth month with her, who was called barren. For with God nothing shall be impossible." (Luke 1:35-37)*

The New Testament also speaks of the Holy Spirit as being equal to Christ. *"I will pray the Father, and he shall give you another Comforter, that he may abide with you for ever; Even the Spirit of truth; whom the world cannot receive, because it seeth him not, neither knoweth him: but ye know him; for he dwelleth with you, and shall be in you. I will not leave you comfortless: I will come to you." (Jn 14:16-18)* Jesus promised the Spirit was going to come to His people. At the same time, He equated the presence of the Spirit with the Father by saying He would not leave them fatherless. Jesus also equated the Spirit with Himself by saying that He, Jesus, would come to them. This is why the indwelling of the Spirit (See Rom 8:9; Eph 1:13,14) is spoken of as Christ being in us (Col 1:27). The Spirit is equal in essence and glory to the Father and the Son. In fact, the Spirit is spoken of as being the Spirit of Christ, the Spirit of God, and Christ in us. *"But ye are not in the flesh, but in the Spirit, if so be that the Spirit of God dwell in you. Now if any man have not the Spirit of Christ, he is none of his. And if Christ be in you, the body is dead because of sin; but the Spirit is life because of righteousness." (Rom 8:9-10)*

These things being so, we are assured that the Spirit of God hovering over the face of the waters which were upon the earth was indeed the Divine Spirit who now indwells the people of God and empowers His church. This Divine Spirit is the giver of life, just as the Son of God gives life (See Jn 1:1-4;5:21-29). *"The Spirit of God hath made me, and the breath of the Almighty hath given me life." (Job 33:4)* (See also Job 26:13; Isa 40:12-14) It is this same Spirit of whom the Psalmist spoke when he said, *"Thou sendest forth thy spirit, they are created: and thou renewest the face of the earth." (Ps 104:30)* The Spirit proceeds from the Father eternally (See Jn 15:26), was sent forth and was active in the creation of the worlds and is sent forth performing creative work even today (See Jn 3:1-8;1Cor 6:9-11; Tit 3:4-8).

Why Is This Important?

One may wonder why a person would take the time to write so many words to establish the truth of the Trinity from the Genesis account of the creation. The answer can be summed up in one word: worship. To worship we must know the truth about God, because worship must be in truth (See Jn 4:24). The creation account bids us to worship one God in three persons, the God who created all things. None other is worthy of our worship. *"Let all the earth fear the LORD: let all the inhabitants of the world stand in awe of him. For he spake, and it was done; he commanded, and it stood fast." (Ps 33:8-9)*

The Tri-unity of God (Trinity)

"For there are three that bear record in heaven, the Father, the Word, and the Holy Ghost: and these three are one." (1 John 5:7)

The doctrine of the Trinity is a doctrine revealed in God's Word, necessary to our faith, and oft disputed. The word trinity simply means, tri-unity or three-in-one. While there is one God who is indivisible, this one God is three persons in one being. Our text above teaches the one true God exists as Father, Word, and Holy Ghost. We often speak of the Father, Son, and Holy Spirit as the three persons of the Godhead. This makes it necessary to define the words Godhead and person. Godhead simply speaks of godhood or the nature and existence of God. When we speak of the three persons of the Godhead, we are declaring that, in the one being God, there who are three distinct yet equal. The Father, Son, and Holy Ghost are not divided but are one even in their being. One is no less God than the other and none is more Divine than another. While they are one, the Father is not these, nor the Son the Spirit, nor the Spirit the Father: the three are distinct yet one. This is impossible to understand and must be received by faith, as God can be known but not comprehended. God fills the universe and exceeds its bounds and can only be known as He reveals Himself to us. Should anyone be able to comprehend God, he would be greater than God; and that is impossible.

The Three Persons Are Each Called God

The Father is God. Notice how God is called the Father of Jesus, the only begotten Son: *"No man hath seen God at any time; the only begotten Son, which is in the bosom of the Father, he hath declared him."* (John 1:18) In John 5:18, Jesus referred to God as His Father, spoke of Him in John 6:27,45,46, and explicitly called God Father in John 8:42,54, and 10:46. The apostle Peter also spoke of God the Father, saying concerning Jesus' resurrection, *"Therefore being by the right hand of God exalted, and having received of the Father the promise of the Holy Ghost, he hath shed forth this, which ye now see and hear."* (Acts 2:33) Above thirty times, Scripture testifies to the Godhood of the Father in the Pauline Epistles (Romans through Hebrews). James, Peter, John, and Jude, in their epistles, speak of God the Father nine times. Finally, in the Revelation, we read, *"Unto him that loved us, and washed us from our sins in his own blood, And hath made us kings and priests unto God and his Father; to him be glory and dominion for ever and ever. Amen."* (Revelation 1:5–6) Because of His preeminent place in recognition and work, we call Him the Father. It does not speak of the Son or the Spirit having beginnings and originating from the Father but rather speaks of the relationships within the Godhead.

The Son is God. One of the most familiar verses read around Christmas time tells us the Son is God and equal to the Father: *"For unto us a child is born, unto us a son is given: and the government shall be upon his shoulder: and his name shall be called Wonderful,*

Counsellor, The mighty God, The everlasting Father, The Prince of Peace." (Isaiah 9:6) Gabriel told Mary the child she bore would be called the Son of the Highest, the very Son of God (Luke 1:32,35), which is the fulfillment of the prophecy of Isaiah chapter nine. The very name given to Jesus, Emmanuel, means "God with us." (Matthew 1:22-23). Jesus proved His Godhood by forgiving

and healing a man crippled with palsy (Matthew 9:1-8). Jesus declared His Godhood by stating He is the Creator who is Lord of the Sabbath day (Mark 2:28). Jesus declared Himself to be

omnipresent (present everywhere), seated at the right hand of the Father while standing on Earth, which omnipresence is an attribute of God alone, and called Himself the only begotten Son (John1:18). This shows us that the Son is God. *"For God sent not his Son into the world to condemn the world; but that the world through him might be saved."* (John 3:17) In fulfillment of the prophecy in Isaiah 9:6, Jesus the Son said He was sent from the Father and thus is God. In John 5:17-18, Jesus speaks of Himself as the Son of God with God as His Father, and the Jews understood Him to claim equality to the Father in Godhood. Philippians 2:5-8 teaches us Christ

Jesus, whom we know is the Son of God, was equal with God before He became a man, and He retains that equality to this day; so, we understand from this that the Son is God. Both Colossians 1:13-19 and Hebrews 1:1-6 teach us the Son is the Creator and thus, God. In 1 John 1:1-3, Jesus is called the Word of life, eternal, and equal to the Father, again showing to us the Godhood of the Son.

The Spirit is God. Just as the Father and the Son are God, the Spirit is God. He is spoken of in Scripture as being the Creator, just as the Father and the Son. *"Thou sendest forth thy spirit, they are created: and thou renewest the face of the earth."* (Psalm 104:30) (See also Genesis 1:1-2; Job 33:4). *"The Spirit of the LORD spake by me, and his word was in my tongue. The God of Israel said, the Rock of Israel spake to me, He that ruleth over men must be just, ruling in the fear of God."* (2 Samuel 23:2–3) David said the Spirit spoke by Him, which was God speaking; by this, we recognize the Spirit is God. The Psalmist also equated the Spirit to God by saying, *"Whither shall I go from thy spirit? or whither shall I flee from thy presence?"* (Psalm 139:7) The prophet Isaiah also implied the Divinity of the Spirit by saying, *"As a beast goeth down into the valley, the Spirit of the LORD caused him to rest: so didst thou lead thy people, to make thyself a glorious name."* (Isaiah 63:14) Notice how Scripture speaks of the Spirit of the LORD and then spoke to God of His personally leading Israel, thus declaring the Deity of the Spirit who is the LORD who led His people. Jesus also taught the Divinity of the Spirit when He said, *"If ye love me, keep my commandments. And I will pray the Father, and he shall give you another Comforter, that he may abide with you for ever; Even the Spirit of truth; whom the world cannot receive, because it seeth him not, neither knoweth him: but ye know him; for he dwelleth with you, and shall be in you. I will not leave you comfortless: I will come to* *you."* (John 14:15–18) This shows us the Spirit who abides with God's people forever is equal to the Son because Jesus said the coming of the Spirit would be His own coming to us. The Son is God, and the Spirit is equal to the Son. Therefore, the Spirit is God. Finally, we can also see this in the Acts where Peter declared that the couple who lied to the Holy Ghost lied to God (Acts 5;1-5).

The Trinity Is a Trinity of Persons and Not of Modes or Manifestations

It is necessary to our study to establish the fact of the Trinity being a Tri-unity of persons in the Godhead rather than three different manifestations or modes of God.

First, let us notice the text Jesus used in one of His first sermons: *"The Spirit of the Lord GOD is upon me; because the LORD hath anointed me to preach good tidings unto the meek;*
he hath sent me to bind up the brokenhearted, to proclaim liberty to the captives, and the opening of the prison to them that are bound." (Isaiah 61:1 cf Luke 4:14-21) We can readily see the Spirit of God, the Son of God, and the Lord who gave the Spirit to the Son. All three of these persons were active at once in this text, thus ruling out the three persons being mere modes in which God manifests Himself at different times.

We can see this even more clearly at the baptism of Jesus. *"And Jesus, when he was baptized, went up straightway out of the water: and, lo, the heavens were opened unto him, and he saw the Spirit of God descending like a dove, and lighting upon him: And lo a voice from heaven, saying, This is my beloved Son, in whom I am well pleased."* (Matthew 3:16–17) This text is strong proof of the Trinity because the Father, Son, and Holy Spirit are in the same place at the same time. The persons of the Trinity simply cannot possibly be merely different modes of Divine manifestation or different manners in which God works. The three are one being, while the distinct persons exist and work together simultaneously.

Jesus' prayers also show us the plurality of persons in the God. After all, how can one pray to another who is simply a manifestation or mode of God who does not show up at the same time or in the same place as the others? Jesus prayed to the Father while in the Garden of Gethsemane. John chapter seventeen is a long prayer of Jesus to His Father. Even if the argument is made that Jesus was praying to the Father as a man and not as God, we cannot separate the deity of Christ from His humanity as if the Son of God left the fleshly Christ to ascend into Heaven and hear the prayer of the Son. It is impossible that Jesus was praying to any other than one who is a Divine person ever distinct from Himself, though one with Him.

A similar argument can be made from Jesus' teaching regarding the sending of the Spirit. *"If ye love me, keep my commandments. And I will pray the Father, and he shall give you another Comforter, that he may abide with you for ever; Even the Spirit of truth; whom the world cannot receive, because it seeth him not, neither knoweth him: but ye know him; for he dwelleth with you, and shall be in you. I will not leave you comfortless: I will come to you."* (John 14:15–18) For the Son to pray to the Father and the Father to send the Spirit, the three persons would necessarily be existent and present simultaneously rather than differing modes or manifestations of God; and the three persons are quite obviously portrayed here as being present simultaneously.

We also read of the Spirit as being the Spirit, the Spirit of God, the Spirit of Christ, and the Spirit of Him that raised up Christ from the dead. *"But ye are not in the flesh, but in the Spirit, if so be that the Spirit of God dwell in you. Now if any man have not the Spirit of Christ, he is none of his. And if Christ be in you, the body is dead because of sin; but the Spirit is life because of righteousness. But if the Spirit of him that raised up Jesus from the dead dwell in you, he that raised up Christ from the dead shall also quicken your mortal bodies by his Spirit that dwelleth in you."* (Romans 8:9–11) Scripture teaches Christ ascended to the right hand of the Father, which

shows us the Father and the Son as both being present in the same place at the same time, which rules out the modal or manifestation idea. The Spirit is ever present within the children of God, according to the promise of John 14:15: *"And I will pray the Father, and he shall give you another Comforter, that he may abide with you for ever ."* (John 14:16) It would be impossible for the Spirit to be with us forever if He had to leave at times to manifest Himself as the Father or the Son. Furthermore, verses nine and ten speak of the Spirit as Christ in us, as well as being the Spirit of the Divine Father who raised up Christ from the dead. Again, in all these things, the various persons of the Trinity necessarily exist, work, and manifest themselves simultaneously. This proves the persons of the Trinity are not various modes or manifestations of the same person. The three persons exist as the one true God while always existing as three persons. This is why we read, *"For there are three that bear record in heaven, the Father, the Word, and the Holy Ghost: and these three are one."* (1 John 5:7)

The Scriptures' witness to the creation also testifies to the Tri-unity of God, as the Father, Son, and Holy Spirit were all simultaneously active in Creation. God sent for His Spirit to do creative work (Psalm 104:30), and one simply does not send Himself but another. Likewise, we read, *"God, who at sundry times and in divers manners spake in time past unto the fathers by the prophets, Hath in these last days spoken unto us by his Son, whom he hath appointed heir of all things, by whom also he made the worlds."* (Hebrews 1:1–2) God not only speaks through His Son, but he made the worlds by the Son, and both were active at the same time. These texts show us once again the Trinity of persons in the Godhead, as the three are one in being and will as well as three persons working together at the same time, which is something modes or manifestations of God cannot or would not do. The Scripture gives abundant witness to the Triune nature of God.

The Practical Effects of The Doctrine of The Trinity

Doctrine Is Practical

Many people have the idea that doctrine is impractical and truly only something academics in ivory towers or intellectuals argue about. Scripture teaches us very differently, however. The great passage concerning the inspiration, authority, and sufficiency of Scripture, 2 Timothy 3:14-17, teaches us that doctrine leads to salvation and sanctification. *"But continue thou in the things which thou hast learned and hast been assured of, knowing of whom thou hast learned them; and that from a child thou hast known the holy scriptures, which are able to make thee wise unto salvation through faith which is in Christ Jesus. All scripture is given by inspiration of God, and is profitable for doctrine, for reproof, for correction, for instruction in righteousness: that the man of God may be perfect, throughly furnished unto all good works." (2 Timothy 3:14–17)* Notice, Scripture leads us to salvation (Salvation is eminently doctrinal. See Romans 6:16-17.), and is profitable to teach us (doctrine), correct us, instruct us, and perfect us. Our salvation and sanctification are based upon Biblical doctrines.

The Trinity and Worship

The doctrine of the Trinity should lead us to worship correctly and deeply. Jesus said, *"Ye worship ye know not what: we know what we worship: for salvation is of the Jews. But the hour cometh, and now is, when the true worshippers shall worship the Father in spirit and in truth: for the Father seeketh such to worship him. God is a Spirit: and they that worship him must worship him in spirit and in truth." (John 4:22–24)* When we know and believe the doctrine of the Trinity, we can worship in truth. The Samaritans did not know God and could not worship in truth. This is not so with us; we know who God is because He reveals Himself to us in the Scriptures.

When we contemplate God being so great that He is of a necessity three persons, we are obligated to worship Him. This greatness of God is such that we cannot search Him out, fathom the depths of His nature and person, nor comprehend Him. *"O the depth of the riches both of the wisdom and knowledge of God! how unsearchable are his judgments, and his ways past finding out! For who hath known the mind of the Lord? or who hath been his counseller? Or who hath first given to him, and it shall be recompensed unto him again? For of him, and through him, and to him, are all things: to whom be glory for ever. Amen." (Romans 11:33–36)*

Furthermore, the truth of the Trinity should lead us to humble and submissive worship. There is nothing at all in the Trinity to lead us to pride. On the other hand, those who insist upon Absolute Oneness or Modalism tend to have pride in themselves. Why not? It seems they have figured God out yet, in doing so, have reduced Him to a manageable size. Thus, their god is comprehensible and can be manipulated to do whatever one wants him to do. This is why the Word of Faith movement with its "Name it and claim it" teachings grew out of the Oneness Pentecostal movement, being something that logically follows a god smaller than the infinite Trinity. This is also why very many Oneness people do not believe there is eternal security for the believer in Christ, they have a small god who needs our help in securing and maintaining our salvation. On the other hand, the Trinitarian faith leads us to worship the One Triune God, who alone can save, seal, and secure His people (Isaiah 45:22-23; John 10:27-30; Ephesians 1:12-14). We cannot comprehend Him nor manipulate Him, but we can certainly bow before Him in faithful, humble, and obedient reverence!

Finally, worship is Triune in that the Father seeks worshipers (John 4:23). The Son came that we might be brought to glory (Ephesians 1:3-14; Hebrews 2:9-10) and offer God spiritual sacrifices (1 Peter 2:5). And the Holy Spirit sanctifies us in our worship and offerings (Romans 15:15-16).

Salvation

If there is any doctrine that is explicitly Trinitarian, it is the doctrine of salvation. Just as the Father, Son, and Holy Spirit were simultaneously personally present and active in Creation, the same is true in salvation. It is only right to affirm once again the reality that there is only one God and one Savior. We read, *"I, even I, am the LORD; And beside me there is no saviour." (Isaiah 43:11)* And again, *"Look unto me, and be ye saved, all the ends of the earth: For I am God, and there is none else." (Isaiah 45:22)* We also read, *"Neither is there salvation in any other: for there is none other name under heaven given among men, whereby we must be saved." (Acts 4:12)* While we affirm there is only one Savior, we also affirm the Trinitarian nature of our Savior and the work of all three persons of the Trinity in our salvation.

The Father sent the Son that we might be saved and can be considered the initiator of our salvation. Jesus' death was according to the will of the Father and was decreed before the Creation. (See Acts 2:23; 4:27-28;2 Timothy 1:8-10 cf Revelation 13:8). There are also approximately forty times in the Gospel According to John alone that God is spoken of as sending the Son. Here are two verses with which we are most familiar: *"For God so loved the world, that he gave his only begotten Son, that whosoever believeth in him should not perish, but have everlasting life. For God sent not his Son into the world to condemn the world; but that the world through him might be saved." (John 3:16–17)* The Father received the offering of Christ for our sins (Ephesians 5:1-2), raised up Christ from the dead (Acts 2:32;13:30; Romans 6:4), and received Him into glory (1 Timothy 3:16; Hebrews 7:26-27;9:11-12,24). It is also the Father who draws sinners (John 6:44) and keeps those who are saved (John 10:27-30).

The Son of God came into the world to save sinners, being sent from the Father. Jesus said, *"this is life eternal, that they might know thee the only true God, and Jesus Christ, whom thou hast sent." (John 17:3)* The Son did the will of the Father, pleased the Father, and offered Himself to the Father in obedience (John 6:38;8:28-29; Ephesians 5:1-2; Philippians 2:5-8). Lest someone object and tell us these verses apply only to the flesh of Christ we add the following:

1. Jesus is one person. He has both Divine and human natures, yet He is one person. We cannot divorce the human and the Divine; Jesus is forever both.
2. Even when speaking of His death, Scripture does not divorce the human from the Divine, saying, "Hereby perceive we the love of God, because he laid down his life for us..." (1 John 3:16) It is true enough that God did not die, yet it is also true that God laid down His life for us in the person of the Son. This cannot be denied. (See also Acts 20:28)

The Son also willingly laid down His life and took it again: *"Therefore doth my Father love me, because I lay down my life, that I might take it again. No man taketh it from me, but I lay it down of myself. I have power to lay it down, and I have power to take it again. This commandment have I received of my Father." (John 10:17–18)* The Son then returned to the Father, prayed to the Father to send the Spirit in the Son's name (John 14:15-18;16:7-16), and promised to come again to take us to ever be with Himself (John 14:1-6).

The Son was anointed with the Spirit, not receiving the Spirit by measure (Luke 4:18; John 3:34; Acts 10:38). The Spirit was in Jesus' going into the wilderness when He was tempted of Satan (Matthew 4:1; Luke 4:1-2). Jesus cast out devils by the Spirit of God (Matthew 12:28). He also ministered in the power of the Spirit (Luke 4:14) and declared the prophecy of Isaiah 61:1 was fulfilled in Him: *"And there was delivered unto him the book of the prophet Esaias. And when he had opened the book, he found the place where it was written, The Spirit of the Lord is upon me, because he hath anointed me to preach the gospel to the poor; he hath sent me to heal the broken-hearted, to preach deliverance to the captives, and recovering of sight to the blind, to set at liberty them that are bruised, to preach the acceptable year of the Lord. And he closed the book, and he gave it again to the minister, and sat down. And the eyes of all them that were in the synagogue were fastened on him. And he began to say unto them, This day is this scripture fulfilled in your ears." (Luke 4:17–21)* It was by the Spirit the Father raised the Son from the dead (Romans 8:11) The Spirit also regenerates those who believe Jesus (John 3:1-16;Titus 3:1-7), baptizing, indwelling, and giving the promise and security of the coming resurrection (Romans 5:5;Ephesians 1:12-14), and abides with the children of God forever (John 14:15-18).

We conclude, then, that salvation is Trinitarian in every way.

Sanctification

The doctrine of sanctification is very practical, as it is the process of God setting us apart for Himself and our yielding to Him in that work of making us holy. We shall now see that sanctification is also Trinitarian in nature.

The Father sanctifies us in Jesus Christ; we read in Jude :1; and Scripture plainly teaches us the Father actively sanctifies His people. Jesus prayed for the Father to sanctify us: *"Sanctify them through thy truth: thy word is truth." (John 17:17)* We are told that we are of God in Christ, who is our sanctification (1 Corinthians 1:30). Chastening comes from the hand of the Father so we will partake in His holiness (Hebrews 12:4-10).

The Son is also active in our sanctification. Jesus said, *"And for their sakes I sanctify myself, that they also might be sanctified through the truth." (John 17:19)* Again, Jesus is our sanctification (1 Corinthians 1:30), and in His name we are set apart as the people of God (1 Corinthians 6:9-11). The Son of God gave Himself for us so He could sanctify us (Ephesians 5:25-27), and present us to Himself holy, unblameable, and unreprovable (Colossians 1:21-22). We are spoken of as being sanctified by the blood of Christ as well as His Word (Hebrews 13:12: Ephesians 5:25-27). There can be no cleansing apart from the blood of Christ, and it is certain the Son of God is active in our sanctification as well.

The regenerating power and indwelling of the Holy Ghost also sanctifies us (1 Corinthians 6:11,18-20; Ephesians 1:13-14), making us a holy temple to the Lord (1 Corinthians 3:17;6:18-20; Ephesians 2:19-22). It is the Spirit within us who makes us holy by producing fruit (Galatians 5:22-23; Ephesians 5:9). It is by the power of the Holy Ghost we please God: *"for the kingdom of God is not meat and drink; but righteousness, and peace, and joy in the Holy Ghost. For he that in these things serveth Christ is acceptable to God, and approved of men." (Romans 14:17–18)* Thus, we again see sanctification is by the Holy Spirit; and it is only by the sanctifying power of the Spirit we retain any iota of goodness: *"That good thing which was committed unto thee keep by the Holy Ghost which dwelleth in us." (2 Timothy 1:14)*

We can conclude that the Father sanctifies us by having sent His Son into the world to die for us and rise again that He, the Son, might sanctify us through His blood and His Word, by the power and presence of the Holy Spirit who lives within us to guide us into all truth(John 16:12-15) and to work in us to will and to do of His good pleasure (Philippians 2:12-13 cf Romans 15:16). Yes, sanctification is a Trinitarian work.

Glorification

When we speak of glorification, we speak of the resurrection of the body and its transformation into the immortal and incorruptible state. We also speak of the resurrection of Jesus from the dead, though his body never saw corruption.

This glorification, Scripture shows, was a Trinitarian act when Jesus was raised and will also be a Trinitarian act when the saints are glorified. Jesus stated He would raise Himself from the dead: *"Therefore doth my Father love me, because I lay down my life, that I might take it again. No man taketh it from me, but I lay it down of myself. I have power to lay it down, and I have power to take it again. This commandment have I received of my Father." (John 10:17–18)* Scripture also tells us the Father raised Jesus from the dead: *"The God of Abraham, and of Isaac, and of Jacob, the God of our fathers, hath glorified his Son Jesus; whom ye delivered up, and denied him in the presence of Pilate, when he was determined to let him go." (Acts 3:13) "who verily was foreordained before the foundation of the world, but was manifest in these last times for you, who by him do believe in God, that raised him up from the dead, and gave him glory; that your faith and hope might be in God." (1 Peter 1:20–21)* Scripture also teaches us Jesus was raised by the Holy Spirit by telling us the Father did not give the Spirit by measure to Him (John 3:34), which lets us know the Spirit never departed from Jesus. Furthermore, Jesus received from the Father the Holy Spirit, which He then poured out upon His saints on Pentecost (Acts 2:32-36), which demonstrates to us that the Spirit which was on Christ without measure and without end was still with and in Him when He ascended. Finally, we find an interesting implication of the Father raising Christ by the Spirit in the following verses: *"But if the Spirit of him that raised up Jesus from the dead dwell in you, he that raised up Christ from the dead shall also quicken your mortal bodies by his Spirit that dwelleth in you." (Romans 8:11) "And God hath both raised up the Lord, and will also raise up us by his own power." (1 Corinthians 6:14)* Our resurrection is to be like Christ's, and our resurrection is of the Lord by His power and His Spirit. This should be no surprise to us, as resurrection is a type of re-creation, and the initial creation was a Trinitarian act also. Thus, we can conclude that Jesus was raised from the dead by His Father, His own will and power, and by the Holy Spirit, thus making Jesus' resurrection a Trinitarian act.

We also read of our glorification as being effected by God in three persons: *"But if the Spirit of him that raised up Jesus from the dead dwell in you, he that raised up Christ from the dead shall also quicken your mortal bodies by his Spirit that dwelleth in you." (Romans 8:11)* Here we find the Father and the Spirit will raise us up. Jesus also promised to raise the dead: *"And this is the will of him that sent me, that every one which seeth the Son, and believeth on him, may have everlasting life: and I will raise him up at the last day." (John 6:40) "Verily, verily, I say unto you, He that heareth my word, and believeth on him that sent me, hath everlasting life, and shall not come into condemnation; but is passed from death unto life. Verily, verily, I say unto you, The hour is coming, and now is, when the dead shall hear the voice of the Son of God: and they that hear shall live. For as the Father hath life in himself; so hath he given to the Son to have life in himself; and hath given him authority to execute judgment also, because he is the Son of man. Marvel not at this: for the hour is coming, in the which all that are in the graves shall hear his voice, and shall come forth; they that have done good, unto the resurrection of life; and they that have done evil, unto the resurrection of damnation. I can of mine own self do nothing: as I hear, I judge: and my judgment is just; because I seek not mine own will, but the will of the Father which hath sent me." (John 5:24–30)* It is interesting to note that Jesus stated He would not be alone in the work of raising the dead because He was working and will work His Father's will. We then conclude that the future resurrection of the saints of God will be a Trinitarian act. Again, Creation was a Trinitarian act, and redemption is a Trinitarian work, so it logically follows that glorification will also be a Trinitarian work.

Objections to The Trinity

In this chapter, we will consider various objections to the doctrine of the Trinity. As we do so, it is important to understand that questions are not necessarily logical or Biblical arguments. Many times, questions are simply designed as a distraction from one's lack of logical and Biblical arguments. At times, these questions are raised to confuse the one contending for the Trinitarian faith. There also seems to be the idea at times that a question demolishes any argument for the Trinity. Reality is quite different, however, and we must resist being provoked to anger or allowing such questions to overwhelm us to the point we concede the argument. The Trinitarian faith is of utmost importance, and we must not yield an iota; this is fundamental to true Christianity.

1. **You worship three gods.**

   This argument is problematic in several ways. First, it ignores the teaching that the Trinity is a Tri-Unity or three Persons who are One God.

   It also erects a straw man and demolishes it, which is logically fallacious. A straw man is a misrepresentation of another's position for the purpose of tearing it down. Sadly, the straw man fallacy does not truly address the argument, which is why it is logically fallacious.

   Finally, this argument is often intellectually and morally dishonest. Many times, those employing this argument know they are misrepresenting what Trinitarians say and choose to utilize this argument anyway.

2. **Jesus praying to His Father was simply Jesus' humanity praying.**

   One thing we as Trinitarians contend for is Jesus being a distinct person from the Father, and we maintain that is obvious because He prayed to His Father. The response given by anti-Trinitarians is that it was Jesus' humanity which was praying.

   This argument neglects the truth of Jesus' being one person in whom Deity and Humanity exists. Scripture tells us the Word, God, was made flesh (John 1:1-3,14), and the fulness of Godhead dwells in Him bodily (Colossians 2:9).

How numerous are the passages that teach us of either the Deity of Christ or the humanity of Jesus! In all of them, we are led to understand Jesus is one person. As a person, whatever Jesus did, He did as one person. Even though we cannot understand it, the person Jesus, although God, died (Acts 20:28;1 John 3:16); and though we can differentiate between the humanity and Deity of Christ, we cannot separate the two. He will forever be both human and Divine, with no mixture nor separation of the two natures.

This argument makes Jesus two persons in one body. If Jesus' flesh was praying to the Father, who was Himself, Jesus is two persons in one body. Ironically, while rejecting the Trinity, those who employ this argument establish a bi-unity. This is a doctrine found nowhere in the Scriptures.

3. **The Father, Son, and Spirit are simply modes in which God manifests Himself.**

This answer will deal with two objections: the first being the statement above and the second being the argument that the word "Trinity" isn't in Scripture.

The word "mode" is not in the Scripture any more than the word "Trinity." Consistency is a jewel! The word "Trinity" does address and deal with the Biblical teaching accurately. "Mode" does not.

Scripture presents God as one God in three persons. This is why Jesus said, *"I and my Father are one." (John 10:30)* It is also why we read, *"For there are three that bear record in heaven, the Father, the Word, and the Holy Ghost: and these three are one." (1 John 5:7)* We also see the distinct persons of the Trinity interacting one with another rather than operating as different modes. Notice how Scripture tells us of the Spirit descending in the visible form of a dove and lighting on the Son while the Father spoke from Heaven regarding the Son at the same time (Matthew 3:13-17). We also see at Jesus' transfiguration the Holy Spirit in the form of the cloud (See Exodus 14:21;40:34;1 Kings 8:10-11;Acts 2:1-4 where the fire and cloud are the presence of the LORD, which is finally shown to be the Holy Spirit baptizing the church as the wind and fire are present.) and the Father speaking again concerning the Son.

Jesus' promise of sending the Spirit also presents to us three persons rather than three modes or manifestations. Jesus said, *"If ye love me, keep my commandments. And I will pray the Father, and he shall give you another Comforter, that he may abide with you for ever; Even the Spirit of truth; whom the world cannot receive, because it seeth him not, neither knoweth him: but ye know him; for he dwelleth with you, and shall be in you. I will not leave you comfortless: I will come to you." (John 14:15–18)* Notice the personal pronouns, I, he, and he. Each personal pronoun references a different person of the Trinity: the Son, the Father, and the Holy Spirit. Yes, the three are one to the degree that it is as if the Father and Son are present with us in the Spirit; yet the Son speaks of the Father and the Spirit as being personally distinct from Himself although of the same being and nature. This personal distinction is very plainly seen in Jesus' prayer in John chapter seventeen: *"These words spake Jesus, and lift up his eyes to heaven, and said, Father, the hour is come; glorify thy Son, that thy Son also may glorify thee: as thou hast given him power over all flesh, that he should give eternal life to as many as thou hast given him. And this is life eternal, that they might know thee the only true God, and Jesus Christ, whom thou hast sent. I have glorified thee on the earth: I have finished the work which thou gavest me to do. And now, O Father, glorify thou me with thine own self with the glory which I had with thee before the world was." (John 17:1–5) "Father, I will that they also, whom thou hast given me, be with me where I am; that they may behold my glory, which thou hast given me: for thou lovedst me before the foundation of the world." (John 17:24)* Jesus' prayer demonstrates that the personal distinction between the Father and the Son existed before the world was, as the Father loved the Son and the Son shared glory with the Father before the foundation of the world. Far from being modes of revelation, the

Father, Son, and Holy Spirit are eternally distinct and Divine persons who are the One True God.

4. **If the Father, Son, and Holy Spirit are not one and the same, why does Scripture say, "God was manifest in the flesh?" (1 Timothy 3:16)**

God was made manifest in the flesh. The verse explains more than simply that God was manifest in the flesh, though. It also tells us of His justification, resurrection, glorification, and ascension. In other words, this verse is telling us of something more than a manifestation: it is speaking of the Deity and work of Christ.

Jesus is God in the flesh. He is the Word, God, made flesh (John 1:1-4,14), who has declared or made known the Father to us. He is the brightness of the glory of God and the express image of His person, showing to us the character and nature of God (Hebrews 1:1-3). While no man has seen God or is able to see God (Exodus 33:20; John 1:18;1 Timothy 1:17; 6:15-16), the Only Begotten Son has made Him known to us, showing us His glory. *"And the Word was made flesh, and dwelt among us, (and we beheld his glory, the glory as of the only begotten of the Father,) full of grace and truth." (John 1:14) "No man hath seen God at any time; the only begotten Son, which is in the bosom of the Father, he hath declared him." (John 1:18)* This is why the eternal Son of God is called "the image of the invisible God" (Colossians 1:15).

While man is unable to see God, He has condescended to come in the person of the Son for us and for our salvation and make Himself known to us. Yes, God was manifest in the flesh.

5. **If you believe in the Trinity, why do we not see three thrones in the end time?**

It is difficult to decide if this is an attempt at a "gotcha" question intended to stump the Trinitarian or if it is a sincere question arising out of an attempt to gain understanding. Motivation notwithstanding, this is a good question, contrary to most questions and objections we have considered. Scripture teaches us there is one God and one King, therefore there will only be one throne. *"And the LORD shall be king over all the earth: In that day shall there be one LORD, and his name one." (Zechariah 14:9)*

I do believe there is a literal throne of God that will be seen, and there is only one. Thirty-nine times the word "throne" is used in the singular in the book of the Revelation. God sits on the throne, and we have every reason to believe and assert this is God the Father, since the Son, the Lamb, sits with Him in His throne (Revelation 3:21;7:17). This throne is called, *"the throne of God and of the Lamb." (Revelation 22:1)*

6. **Why is Jesus called the everlasting Father if the Father, Son, and Spirit are not one and the same person?**

"For unto us a child is born, unto us a Son is given: And the government shall be upon his shoulder: And his name shall be called Wonderful, Counseller, The mighty God, The everlasting Father, The Prince of Peace." (Isaiah 9:6)

Here is an interesting thing: never in His life and ministry was Jesus called "the everlasting Father." We can take one of two approaches to this, then: we can erroneously declare that Scripture has an error in it, or we can consider this in light of Scripture and understand it is a figure of speech is teaching us of the unity existing between the Father and the Son. After all, Jesus stated that He is one with the Father (John 10:30). We have also seen that Jesus has revealed the Father to us (John 1:18), which is why He said, *"he that hath seen me hath seen the Father; and how sayest thou then, Shew us the Father?" (John 14:9)* We have already established the personal distinction between the Father and the Son, so we are bound by reason and Scripture to declare this to be a figure of speech teaching us of the Deity of Christ and His essential unity with the Father.

7. **The Bible says God is one.**

Yes, it does. No Trinitarian denies that God is one. The very word, "Trinity," means "Tri-unity" or three in one. Again, Trinitarians believe in the three Divine Persons being the One True God.

8. **Why do you speak of Father, Son, and Holy Ghost as distinct when the Bible says God has one name?**

This question seems to stem from a misunderstanding or misapplication of the Biblical usage of "name" in relation to God. God has a name, and has revealed it to us: *"And Moses said unto God, Behold, when I come unto the children of Israel, and shall say unto them, The God of your fathers hath sent me unto you; and they shall say to me, What is his name? what shall I say unto them? And God said unto Moses, I AM THAT I AM: and he said, Thus shalt thou say unto the children of Israel, I AM hath sent me unto you. And God said moreover unto Moses, Thus shalt thou say unto the children of Israel, The LORD God of your fathers, the God of Abraham, the God of Isaac, and the God of Jacob, hath sent me unto you: this is my name for ever, and this is my memorial unto all generations." (Exodus 3:13–15) "And God spake unto Moses, and said unto him, I am the LORD: and I appeared unto Abraham, unto Isaac, and unto Jacob, by the name of God Almighty, but by my name JEHOVAH was I not known to them." (Exodus 6:2–3)* God's name is, "I AM" or "JEHOVAH." He teaches His children to address Him as, "our Father" (Matthew 6:9-13).

There is more to a name than simply what one is called, however, because one's name is his reputation. This is why we read, *"A good name is rather to be chosen than great riches, And loving favour rather than silver and gold." (Proverbs 22:1)* In Exodus chapter three, seen above, we find the LORD stated similarly when He told us His name is "I AM" and that it is also His memorial. God's name is His fame. God's name is His honor and His glory. Many, many times Scripture tells us of God working for His name's sake. He used Isaiah to write, *"I am the LORD: that is my name: And my glory will I not give to another, Neither my praise to graven images." (Isaiah 42:8)* Having already established the truthfulness of the Trinitarian doctrine, I shall only state that the name of God is the name of the Trinity. This is why there is a singular name while the three persons are called by name; they are the One True God: *"Go ye therefore, and teach all nations, baptizing them in the name of the Father, and of the Son, and of the Holy Ghost:" (Matthew 28:19)*

Furthermore, the use of the word, "name," refers to authority. This is why law enforcement officers once would say, "Stop, in the name of the law!" It was not because one needed to stop and say, "In the name of the law." We all know that is foolish, so why do some refuse to acknowledge the foolishness of demanding something be done using the words, "In the name of the Lord Jesus," as though it were a required formula or powerful incantation? Many times, in the Old Testament, we find men speaking in the name of the LORD. Priests were to minister in the name of the LORD and true prophets spoke in the name of the LORD (Deuteronomy 18:7,22). David faced and conquered Goliath in the name of the LORD (1 Samuel 17:45), and later said, *"We will rejoice in thy salvation, And in the name of our God we will set up our banners: The LORD fulfil all thy petitions." (Psalm 20:5)* Solomon built a house to the name of the LORD (1 Kings 5:1-5) and for the name of the LORD (1 Kings 8:1-20). David blessed the people in the name of the LORD (1 Chronicles 16:2). David also said, *"I will praise the LORD according to his righteousness: And will sing praise to the name of the LORD most High." (Psalm 7:17)* The heathen will fear the name of the LORD (Psalm 102:15). Jesus came and will return in the name of the LORD (Psalm 118:26; Matthew 23:39). Israel worshiped in Jerusalem, giving thanks unto the name of the LORD (Psalm 122:4); and David said, *"Our help is in the name of the LORD, Who made heaven and earth." (Psalm 124:8)* We know also that *"The name of the LORD is a strong tower: The righteous runneth into it, and is safe." (Proverbs 18:10)* We also read of the name of the LORD coming with anger and indignation (Isaiah 30:27-28). We also understand that *"And it shall come to pass, that whosoever shall call on the name of the LORD shall be delivered..." (Joel 2:32)* In none of these instances is it absolutely necessary that we say, "In the name of the LORD." Instead, we see that the name of the LORD is His reputation, glory, fame, and authority. In fact, God's name stands for His nature and character just as our name carries the reputation of our nature and character. God's being, character, nature, and glory are one. Thus, we read of the singular name of the LORD.

9. **Why, then, does the New Testament speak so much of Jesus' name?**

This is indeed an important question. First, let us bear in mind all that has been shown from Scripture in answer to the previous question. Then, we must recognize that the very name of Jesus is the name of the LORD. Jesus means, "The LORD saves," or "JEHOVAH saves." God has plainly stated there is no Savior other than Himself: *"I am the LORD, and there is none else, There is no God besides me: I girded thee though thou hast not known me:" (Isaiah 45:5) "Look unto me, and be ye saved, all the ends of the earth: For I am God, and there is none else." (Isaiah 45:22)* We know Jesus is the LORD of whom Isaiah spoke in chapter forty because He is said to be the one promised (Isaiah 40:1-5; Matthew 3:1-3; John 1:15). The name of Jesus is the name of the LORD.

We must not fail, however, to recall that there are more Scriptures having bearing on this subject, which Scriptures tell us Jesus came in the name of the Father. *"I am come in my Father's name, and ye receive me not: if another shall come in his own name, him ye will receive."*

(John 5:43) He *also did His works in the Father's name (John 10:25)*. Jesus also prayed for the glory of the Father's name: *"Father, glorify thy name. Then came there a voice from heaven, saying, I have both glorified it, and will glorify it again." (John 12:28)* He also promised to answer prayer to the glory of the Father's name: *"And whatsoever ye shall ask in my name, that will I do, that the Father may be glorified in the Son." (John 14:13)* Jesus likewise asked the Father to keep His people through the name of the Father (John 17:11). Then, He promised the Father would send the Holy Spirit in Jesus' name (John 14:26). These things are important to note because Jesus' name is not exclusive in the New Testament. It is true He is our only Savior: *"Neither is there salvation in any other: for there is none other name under heaven given among men, whereby we must be saved." (Acts 4:12)* This does not mean one must exclude the Father and the Spirit from the salvation act, especially when we have already demonstrated from Scripture that salvation is explicitly a Trinitarian work. It simply means Jesus Christ is the only way of salvation, as He said: *"I am the way, the truth, and the life: no man cometh unto the Father, but by me." (John 14:6)*

Why Jesus' name, then? Jesus' name is emphasized because the Father sent the Son into the world that we might live through Him (1 John 4:9-10). Through His sinless life, offering Himself to the Father as the sacrifice for our sins, rising from the dead, and ascending to the right hand of the Father to be our one mediator (1 Timothy 2:5-6; Hebrews 7:23-28), Jesus is our only way to be saved. It is only through Him we can pray (John 14:12-13); it is only through Him we have access by the Holy Spirit to the Father (Ephesians 2:18); it is only through Jesus we can worship God acceptably in the Spirit (Romans 15:15-16;Ephesians 2:14-22;1 Peter 2:5); and it is only through Him the full Godhead of Father, Son, and Holy Ghost will be forever exalted and glorified (Philippians 2:9-11;1 Corinthians 15:22-28). The name of Jesus is exalted because He God raised Him up to be our Prince and Savior who gives repentance and remission of sins, and the Holy Ghost is witness of this (Acts 5:30-32); and this is a trinity of Trinitarian verses!

10. The Trinity is a Roman Catholic invention and was not taught before the Council of Nicaea.

When was the word Trinity first used? It has been claimed that Tertullian coined the term in the late 2nd or early 3rd century. It has also been claimed that Tertullian was a Roman Catholic and the Roman Catholics defined the Trinity at the Council of Nicaea in AD325. The Roman Catholic Church cannot truly be said to have existed until AD325 or later (Leo, the first pope, was not around until the fifth century, so a fourth century date is generously early.), so Tertullian could not have been a Roman Catholic. Tertullian also did not originate the term, Trinity.

The first instance we find in the Ante-Nicene Fathers is from Theophilus of Antioch, who said, "In like manner also the three days which were before the luminaries, are types of the Trinity, of God, and His Word, and His wisdom." [A.D. 115–181.] (Editor's Note: "Τριάδος. [The earliest use of this word "Trinity." It seems to have been used by this writer in his lost works, also; and, as a learned friends suggests, the use he makes of it is familiar. He does not lug it in as something novel: "types of the Trinity," he says, illustrating an accepted word, not introducing a new one.]")[15] Notice how the editors show us Theophilus' use of the word Trinity was a familiar usage and not novel. After all, he did not have to define his term here. Why? Because it could be assumed he and his audience were already familiar with it.

There was also Clement of Alexandria [A.D. 153–217.], who said, "I understand nothing else than the Holy Trinity to be meant; for the third is the Holy Spirit, and the Son is the second, by whom all things were made according to the

---

15 Alexander Roberts, James Donaldson, and A. Cleveland Coxe, eds., Fathers of the Second Century: Hermas, Tatian, Athenagoras, Theophilus, and Clement of Alexandria (Entire), vol. 2, The Ante-Nicene Fathers (Buffalo, NY: Christian Literature Company, 1885).

will of the Father."[16] Clement very explicitly expresses his Trinitarian faith by declaring the Father, then the second person the Son, and the third person the Holy Spirit while using the singular term, "Trinity."

I realize this will not serve to convince folks whose minds are already settled about what they believe. Historical accuracy is a must, however, and honesty demands we be historically accurate.

11. If the Father is God, as well as the Son and the Holy Ghost, which one do you call the Almighty?

This objection is one based upon the straw man fallacy which declares Trinitarians believe in three gods. Since that fallacy is a false

---

[16] Clement of Alexandria, "The Stromata, or Miscellanies," in Fathers of the Second Century: Hermas, Tatian, Athenagoras, Theophilus, and Clement of Alexandria (Entire), ed. Alexander Roberts, James Donaldson, and A. Cleveland Coxe, vol. 2, The Ante-Nicene Fathers (Buffalo, NY: Christian Literature Company, 1885), 468.

representation of Trinitarian doctrine, this objection is irrelevant and has no bearing at all on the subject.

It does bear answering, however, simply to show the folly of the argument. Since we have already shown from the Scripture the truth of the doctrine of the Trinity, let it suffice us to remember Trinitarian doctrine is the true doctrine of the One True God of Scripture. Since Trinitarians believe in one God and all three Persons of the Trinity are the One True God, we can say that the Father is Almighty, the Son is Almighty, and the Spirit is Almighty; for, "these three are one." (1 John 5:7) They are not separated but are One Almighty.

Furthermore, this objection commits the mistake of trying to reduce the eternal by dividing it by three. However, eternity is infinity; and infinity divided by three still equals infinity. Thus, their argument fails once again.

In short, the Trinity is three Persons who are one in essence and equal in power and glory. We can rightly, Biblically, and logically call all three Persons the Almighty.

Why Modalism and Absolute Oneness Are Heretical

"For there are three that bear record in heaven, the Father, the Word, and the Holy Ghost: and these three are one." (1 John 5:7)

"If ye love me, keep my commandments. And I will pray the Father, and he shall give you another Comforter, that he may abide with you for ever; Even the Spirit of truth; whom the world cannot receive, because it seeth him not, neither knoweth him: but ye know him; for he dwelleth with you, and shall be in you. I will not leave you comfortless: I will come to you." (John 14:15–18)

"These things have I spoken unto you, being yet present with you." (John 14:25)

Modalism and Absolute Oneness both teach not only that there is one God, but also that God is one person. This is contrary to the plain teaching of the Scripture, which presents to us God as Trinity or one God who is three persons. Modalism teaches that God is one person who manifests Himself in different modes or under different titles; and Absolute Oneness is similar, declaring there is absolutely one person who holds all titles simultaneously while manifesting himself under those titles. Ultimately, there is very little difference between the two doctrines, so I will deal with them as one.

Here are some quotes from Modalist statements of faith:

- "There is only ONE GOD: the Creator of the heavens and the earth, and of all mankind. This One God, the I AM, is manifested (revealed) to mankind as FATHER (Creator), SON (Savior, 1 Jn.5:20), and HOLY GHOST (indwelling Spirit, Rom. 8:11). God is a Spirit (John 4:24), the Eternal One, the Creator of all things, and of all men. Thus, making Him their Father (through creation, Malachi 2:10). The LORD is the FIRST and the LAST, and beside Him there is no God (Isa. 44:6)."[17]
- "We believe in the One ever-living, eternal God; infinite in power, holy in nature, attributes and purpose, and possessing absolute, indivisible Deity. This one true God has revealed Himself as Father in creation, through the Son in redemption, and as the Holy Ghost by emanation (I Corinthians 8:6; Ephesians 4:6; II Corinthians 5:19; Joel 2:28) … This one True God manifested Himself in the Old Testament in divers ways, in the Son while He walked among men; as the Holy Ghost after the ascension.[18]

---

[17] https://aljc.org/doctrinal-statement-copy/ (Accessed 02/24/2025)

[18] https://aljc.org/articles-of-faith/ (Accessed 02/24/2025)

- There is one God, who has revealed Himself as Father; through His Son, in redemption; and as the Holy Spirit, by emanation. Jesus Christ is God manifested in flesh. He is both God and man. (See Deuteronomy 6:4; Ephesians 4:4-6; Colossians 2:9; I Timothy 3:16.)[19]

History shows Modalism was first taught in the second century AD by one Noetus, of whom Novation said, "Now, that *Noetus* affirms that the Son and Father are the same, no one is ignorant. But he makes his statement thus: 'When indeed, then, the Father had not been born, He *yet* was justly styled Father; and when it pleased Him to undergo generation, having been begotten, He Himself became His own Son, not another's.'[20]" We read also of one Sabellius who taught a doctrine similar to that of Noetus: "But some treat the Holy Trinity in an awful manner, when they confidently

---

[19] https://upci.org/our-beliefs/ (Accessed 02/24/2025)

[20] Hippolytus of Rome, "The Refutation of All Heresies," in *Fathers of the Third Century: Hippolytus, Cyprian, Novatian, Appendix*, ed. Alexander Roberts, James Donaldson, and A. Cleveland Coxe, trans. J. H. MacMahon, vol. 5, The Ante-Nicene Fathers (Buffalo, NY: Christian Literature Company, 1886), 127–128.

assert that there are not three persons, and introduce (the idea of) a person devoid of subsistence. Wherefore we clear ourselves of Sabellius, who says that the Father and the Son are the same. For he holds that the Father is He who speaks, and that the Son is the Word that abides in the Father, and becomes manifest at the time of the creation, and thereafter reverts to God on the fulfilling of all things. The same affirmation he makes also of the Spirit. We forswear this, because we believe that three persons—namely, Father, Son, and Holy Spirit—are declared to possess the one Godhead: for the one divinity showing itself forth according to nature in the Trinity establishes the oneness of the nature; and thus there is a (divinity that is the) property of the Father, according to the word, 'There is one God the Father;' and there is a divinity hereditary in the Son, as it is written, 'The Word was God;' and there is a divinity present according to nature in the Spirit—to wit, what subsists as the Spirit of God—according to Paul's statement, 'Ye are the temple of God, and the Spirit of God dwelleth in you.'[21]" Another said, "Sabellius...blasphemes in saying that the

---

[21] Pseudo-Gregory Thaumaturgus, "A Sectional Confession of Faith," in *Fathers of the Third Century: Gregory Thaumaturgus, Dionysius the Great, Julius Africanus, Anatolius and Minor Writers, Methodius, Arnobius*, ed. Alexander Roberts, James Donaldson, and A. Cleveland Coxe, trans. S. D. F. Salmond, vol. 6, The Ante-Nicene Fathers (Buffalo, NY: Christian Literature Company, 1886), 42.

Son Himself is the Father, and *vice versa*[22]." We also read, "For Sabellius, the God of Hellenistic philosophy, the absolute and unlimited Being, is the same as the God of the Church. The three Persons which the historical experience of the Church affirmed are just three masks, three different modes of appearance and activity of the one God: specifically, God appears and acts in the Old Testament as Father, in the New Testament as Son, in the life of the Church as Holy Spirit.[23]"

This doctrine is called Modalism because it teaches the one God manifests Himself in different modes or masks. Another way it is presently described is, one God but three different titles.

As one can see, this doctrine was immediately opposed as heresy, and it should be opposed as such today. We shall now see why we should oppose it.

---

[22] Dionysius of Rome, "Against the Sabellians," in *Fathers of the Third and Fourth Centuries: Lactantius, Venantius, Asterius, Victorinus, Dionysius, Apostolic Teaching and Constitutions, Homily, and Liturgies*, ed. Alexander Roberts, James Donaldson, and A. Cleveland Coxe, vol. 7, The Ante-Nicene Fathers (Buffalo, NY: Christian Literature Company, 1886), 365.

[23] Christos Yannaras, *Elements of Faith: An Introduction to Orthodox Theology*, trans. Keith Schram (Edinburgh: T&T Clark, 2006), 23.

Why Modalism and Absolute Oneness Are Heresy

- They misrepresent Biblical Trinitarian doctrine as teaching three gods as well as teaching three separate persons. (Note: the three Divine Persons are distinct but not separate.)
- Modalism presents God as one who changes. Instead of being the same yesterday, today, and forever (*Malachi 3:6; Hebrews 13:8*).
- Both doctrines present to us a diminished and weak god whose power and glory are too small to be three persons; therefore he can only change from one to the other in appearance and title.
- Modalism presents to us a god who lies, because God said He does not change, while Modalists teach God does change from Father to Son to Spirit.
- Both doctrines deny the very Word of God that teaches God is three persons in one being. (*1 John 5:7; John 14:15-25;2 Corinthians 13:14*)
- These erroneous doctrines teach Jesus was literally begotten in the flesh by the Father and the Holy Ghost, failing to understand Jesus' conception was not a mere carnal conception but a special creative work of God, as Jesus is the second Adam (Compare *Genesis 2:7* and *Luke 1:35*.).[24]

---

[24] "If God and the Holy Ghost are two separate persons, which was the Father of Christ? Matthew

- Both present an illogical and irrational god.
    - These two doctrines present a Father who is His own Son and Son who is His own Father as well as being the Spirit. This is both impossible and irrational. An impossible and irrational god does not exist; therefore, the god of Modalism and Absolute Oneness does not exist, and those who teach them preach a different Jesus than the Bible teaches.
    - While not necessarily using these words, both teach the Father sent Himself in the Son, who obeyed Himself as the Father, offered Himself as a sacrifice to Himself

---

1:20 says that the Holy Ghost was the Father, while Romans 15:6, II Corinthians 11:31, and Ephesians 1:3 say that God was the Father. There is no contradiction when we realize that God the Father and the Holy Ghost are one and the same Spirit. Matthew 10:20; Ephesians 4:4; I Corinthians 3:16." From https://christianity.stackexchange.com/questions/32960/what-churches-identify-themselves-as-being-modalist (Accessed 02/24/2025)

as the Father, was raised by Himself as both Father and Spirit, ascended to Himself and sits at His own right hand as the Son of His Father who is Himself, is mediator and intercessor between Himself and man, and prayed to Himself as the Father and sent Himself as the Spirit from Himself.

- Both present to us a mentally ill god who speaks to himself, pretends there is a god other than himself to whom he prays although he is himself, and declares there is a god other than himself who indwells his people although he is the same god. Again, such an irrational god is impossible and non-existent and is thus different from the God of Scripture and the Jesus of the gospel.
- Both doctrines teach a god who is not three persons yet manifests himself as three personalities as one lights on another and one speaks of another, saying, "Can Trinitarians show that three divine persons were present when Jesus was baptized by John? Absolutely not. The one, omnipresent *God used three simultaneous manifestations. Only one divine person was present*--Jesus Christ the Lord."[25] This is irrational and a plain distortion of the Scriptures.

25

https://christianity.stackexchange.com/questions/32

- *Luke 4:1* says Jesus was filled with the Holy Ghost. If Modalism were true Jesus would have been filled with Himself, which is neither logical nor complimentary.
- Both teachings distort the gospel by confusing the persons of the Father, Son, and Holy Spirit.
    - The Father sent the Son into the world to die for our sins and rise again. *John 3:16-17; 6:33-41*
    - The Son ascended to Heaven to sit on the right hand of the Father as our mediator and to intercede with the Father for us. *Mark 16:19; Acts 2:34; 7:55-56; Romans 8:34; Hebrews 10:12.*
    - The Son prayed to the Father and the Father sent the Spirit in the Son's name.
        - The sending of the Holy Spirit *Luke 11:13; John 14:15-25; Acts 2:33*
        - The Spirit sent into the hearts of believers *Romans 5:5;2 Corinthians 1:21-22; 5:5;Galatians 4:6; Ephesians 1:12-14;1 John 3:24; 4:13*
        - By the Spirit we approach the Father through the Son. *John 3:5,16; Ephesians 2:18; Romans*

960/what-churches-identify-themselves-as-being-modalist (Accessed 02/24/2025)

8:26-27 and *Jude 1:20 cf Hebrews 10:19-22*

Such muddled doctrine easily leads to confusion concerning the gospel of Christ. In fact, this doctrine is a distortion and misrepresentation of the gospel because of its misrepresentation of God. Who did what? To whom should we pray? Who died for whom and who sent whom? And who is at work in the world and in God's children? These have no clear and plain answer in either theology, whereas Trinitarian theology answers them precisely.

- Finally, Modalism and Absolute Oneness are heresy because they blaspheme God through misrepresenting Him as He reveals Himself to us in Scripture and diminishing His glory and greatness as a result.

Modalism and Absolute Oneness Are Damnable Heresies

A damnable heresy is one that deserves condemnation and makes those holding it liable to condemnation. This is not a claim to make lightly or take lightly; and I do not make this claim carelessly.

Scripture says, *"I have not written unto you because ye know not the truth, but because ye know it, and that no lie is of the truth. Who is a liar but he that denieth that Jesus is the Christ? He is antichrist, that denieth the Father and the Son. Whosoever denieth the Son, the same hath not the Father: (but) he that acknowledgeth the Son hath the Father also." (1 John 2:21–23)* Modalism and Absolute Oneness deny Jesus the Christ by declaring Him to be the Father and the Spirit, denying His eternal Sonship as the only begotten of the Father. In so doing, according to the text above, this is also a denial and rejection of the Father. This is damnable because it leaves those who hold this doctrine in a very precarious spiritual position.

I will not claim that every person who holds to Absolute Oneness or Modalism is lost, but will state the following:

1. If they are truly saved God will chasten them and bring them to repentance and the truth. *Hebrews 12:4-11.*
2. If they are saved and refuse to repent when chastened God will take them out of this life for this sinfulness. *1 Corinthians 11:30-32 cf 1 John 5:16*
3. Those who hold this doctrine and never repent and never experience chastening never knew God at all. *"They went out from us, but they were not of us; for if they had been of us, they would no doubt have continued with us: but they went out, that they might be made manifest that they were not all of us. But ye have an unction from the Holy One, and ye know all things. I have not written unto you because ye know not the truth, but because ye know it, and that no lie is of the truth. Who is a liar but he that denieth that Jesus is the Christ? He is antichrist, that denieth the*

Father and the Son. Whosoever denieth the Son, the same hath not the Father: (but) he that acknowledgeth the Son hath the Father also." (1 John 2:19–23)

I realize these are very serious claims, and state again that I do not make them carelessly but with a heavy heart. We have been very plainly warned against heretics who deny the Lord. God's Word says, *"But there were false prophets also among the people, even as there shall be false teachers among you, who privily shall bring in damnable heresies, even denying the Lord that bought them, and bring upon themselves swift destruction. And many shall follow their pernicious ways; by reason of whom the way of truth shall be evil spoken of." (2 Peter 2:1–2)* Not only are their doctrines and ways damnable and destructive, but we are commanded to separate from them. *"Whosoever transgresseth, and abideth not in the doctrine of Christ, hath not God. He that abideth in the doctrine of Christ, he hath both the Father and the Son. If there come any unto you, and bring not this doctrine, receive him not into your house, neither bid him God speed:" (2 John 9–10)* This is not to say we are to mistreat them and abuse them. We certainly are not to be bitter toward them. We should love them enough to warn them. We should pity them and pray for their repentance. The last thing we should wish upon anyone is for them to experience the pains of chastisement or death; and we certainly should never desire for someone to die without believing the true gospel of Jesus Christ.

To sum this up, Modalism and Absolute Oneness are heresies because both deny the Father and the Son, misrepresent God, distort the gospel, and condemn souls. Let us pray for those who hold these doctrines!

A Historical Defense of The Doctrine of The Trinity from The First Two Centuries AD

Did The Doctrine of The Trinity Originate in The Roman Catholic Church? (An Inquiry into The Ante-Nicene Fathers of The First and Second Centuries)

I. Who Were the Ante-Nicene Fathers?

The Ante-Nicene Fathers were ancient Christians of influence who lived before (Thus we have the "ante".) the Council of Nicaea, which was held in AD325.

My inquiry is specifically into the Ante-Nicene Fathers of the first two centuries. The reason for studying within these first two centuries is because heresies seem to have become much more rampant afterward. Even more importantly, those of the first two centuries were much closer to the times of the apostles, and we should expect them to have held many of the same doctrines as the apostles.

It is to be noted that, among these writers were two who had very close contact with the apostles. Polycarp was converted under the ministry of the apostle John. "Irenæus was his disciple, and tells us that 'Polycarp was instructed by the apostles, and was brought into contact with many who had seen Christ'"[26] "Irenæus gives us one of the very few portraits of an apostolic man which are to be found in antiquity, in a few sentences which are a picture: 'I could describe the very place in which the blessed Polycarp sat and taught; his going out and coming in; the whole tenor of his life; his personal appearance; how he would speak of the conversations he had held with John and with others who had seen the Lord. How did he make mention of their words and of whatever he had heard from them respecting the Lord.'"[27] It is to be

---

[26] Alexander Roberts, James Donaldson, and A. Cleveland Coxe, eds., "Introductory Note to the Epistle of Polycarp to the Philippians," in *The Apostolic Fathers with Justin Martyr and Irenaeus*, vol. 1, The Ante-Nicene Fathers (Buffalo, NY: Christian Literature Company, 1885), 32.

[27] Alexander Roberts, James Donaldson, and A. Cleveland Coxe, eds., "Introductory Note to the Epistle of Polycarp to the Philippians," in *The Apostolic Fathers with Justin Martyr and Irenaeus*, vol. 1, The Ante-

expected that we could learn much of the apostolic teaching from reading what such men had to say.

Another reason for searching these writings concerning the doctrine of the Trinity is the relevance of this doctrine to their times, as these men dealt with major Christological heresies in their day. They contended with the Gnostics and Docetists, who held many different ideas about Christ. Some of them held him to be some sort of exalted man, others a created god, while others considered Jesus to be one of many gods, and others said Christ appeared to have come in the flesh but did not truly do so. The doctrine of the Deity of Christ as well as the Trinity looms largely in relation to such heresies. For this reason, we inquire into the beliefs of these ancient Christians concerning the Trinity.

It must also be stated that I do not agree with everything these writers believed. This is not an endorsement of their doctrine but a historical survey of their belief in the Trinity.

II. What Did the Ante-Nicene Fathers of The First Two Centuries Believe About God?

Nicene Fathers (Buffalo, NY: Christian Literature Company, 1885), 31.

As we study the writings of this period in history, we must briefly define the doctrine of the Trinity so we can specify what we are seeking. The word Trinity simply means three in one or tri-unity. The doctrine of the Trinity, while being nuanced in theology texts, can be simply stated as the belief that there is one being who is God and He is three persons, with person being defined as one with defined characteristics as well as intellect and will. It is this belief we are seeking to ascertain what these early Christians believed.

The Ante-Nicene Fathers Believed in One God

Ignatius lived AD 30-107 and is said to have been a disciple under the guidance of the apostle John.

- "But our Physician is the only true God, the unbegotten and unapproachable, the Lord of all, the Father and Begetter of the only-begotten Son. We have also as a Physician the Lord our God, Jesus the Christ, the only-begotten Son and Word, before time began, but who afterwards became also man, of Mary the virgin. For "the Word was made flesh."[11] Being incorporeal, He was in the body; being impassible, He was in a passible body; being immortal, He was in a mortal body; being life, He became subject to corruption, that He might free our souls from death and corruption, and heal them, and might restore them to health, when they were diseased with ungodliness and wicked lusts.[28]" [A.D. 30–107.]

It is quite easily noted that Ignatius believed there was only one true God.

- "Since, also, there is but one unbegotten Being, God, even the Father; and one only-begotten Son, God, the Word and man; and one Comforter, the Spirit of truth; and also one preaching, and one faith, and one baptism; and one Church which the holy apostles established from one end of the earth to the other by the blood of Christ, and by their own sweat and toil; it behoves you also, therefore, as "a peculiar people, and a holy nation,"[3] to perform all things with harmony in Christ.[29]"

---

[28] Ignatius of Antioch, "The Epistle of Ignatius to the Ephesians," in *The Apostolic Fathers with Justin Martyr and Irenaeus*, ed. Alexander Roberts, James Donaldson, and A. Cleveland Coxe, vol. 1, The Ante-Nicene Fathers (Buffalo, NY: Christian Literature Company, 1885), 52.

[29] Ignatius of Antioch, "The Epistle of Ignatius to the Philadelphians," in *The Apostolic Fathers with Justin Martyr and Irenaeus*, ed. Alexander Roberts, James Donaldson, and A. Cleveland Coxe, vol. 1, The Ante-

Again, we find Ignatius plainly declaring his belief that there is only one being who is God.

- "If any one preaches the one God of the law and the prophets, but denies Christ to be the Son of God, he is a liar, even as also is his father the devil, and is a Jew falsely so called, being possessed of[6] mere carnal circumcision. If any one confesses Christ Jesus the Lord, but denies the God of the law and of the prophets, saying that the Father of Christ is not the Maker of heaven and earth, he has not continued in the truth any more than his father the devil, and is a disciple of Simon Magus, not of the Holy Spirit. If any one says there is one God, and also confesses Christ Jesus, but thinks the Lord to be a mere man, and not the only-begotten God, and Wisdom, and the Word of God, and deems Him to consist merely of a soul and body, such an one is a serpent, that preaches deceit and error for the destruction of men. And such a man is poor in understanding, even as by name he is an Ebionite.[9]

Nicene Fathers (Buffalo, NY: Christian Literature Company, 1885), 81.

Here Ignatius speaks plainly of the Old Testament teaching of monotheism, contending for the truth of there being only one God.

Irenaeus lived AD120-202 and was, as previously stated, a disciple of the apostle John. Most of his ministry was in Lyons, France.

- "And others of them, with great craftiness, adapted such parts of Scripture to their own figments, lead away captive from the truth those who do not retain a stedfast faith in one God, the Father Almighty, and in one Lord Jesus Christ, the Son of God.[30]"

Irenaeus simply states his belief in the reality of there being one God.

- "But if the Word of the Father who descended is the same also that ascended, He, namely, the Only-begotten Son of the only God, who, according to the good pleasure of the Father, became flesh for

---

[30] Irenaeus of Lyons, "Irenæus against Heresies," in *The Apostolic Fathers with Justin Martyr and Irenaeus*, ed. Alexander Roberts, James Donaldson, and A. Cleveland Coxe, vol. 1, The Ante-Nicene Fathers (Buffalo, NY: Christian Literature Company, 1885), 320.

the sake of men, the apostle certainly does not speak regarding any other, or concerning any Ogdoad, but respecting our Lord Jesus Christ."[31]

Once again Irenaeus affirms his belief in one God by speaking of "the only God."

- "The Church, though dispersed throughout the whole world, even to the ends of the earth, has received from the apostles and their disciples this faith: [She believes] in one God, the Father Almighty, Maker of heaven, and earth, and the sea, and all things that are in them; and in one Christ Jesus, the Son of God, who became incarnate for our salvation; and in the Holy Spirit, who proclaimed through the prophets the dispensations of God, and the advents, and the birth from a virgin, and the passion, and the resurrection from the

---

[31] Irenaeus of Lyons, "Irenæus against Heresies," in *The Apostolic Fathers with Justin Martyr and Irenaeus*, ed. Alexander Roberts, James Donaldson, and A. Cleveland Coxe, vol. 1, The Ante-Nicene Fathers (Buffalo, NY: Christian Literature Company, 1885), 329.

dead, and the ascension into heaven in the flesh of the beloved Christ Jesus, our Lord, and His [future] manifestation from heaven in the glory of the Father "to gather all things in one," and to raise up anew all flesh of the whole human race, in order that to Christ Jesus, our Lord, and God, and Saviour, and King, according to the will of the invisible Father, "every knee should bow, of things in heaven, and things in earth, and things under the earth, and that every tongue should confess" to Him[32]"

This ancient confession of faith is stated by Irenaeus to be the truth he and all saints had received from the apostles. Considering his times, it is reasonable to believe he literally heard this truth from the apostles. What did the apostles teach? First, they taught there is one God.

- "But there is one only God, the Creator— He who is above every Principality, and Power, and Dominion, and Virtue: He is Father, He is God, He the Founder, He the

---

[32] Irenaeus of Lyons, "Irenæus against Heresies," in *The Apostolic Fathers with Justin Martyr and Irenaeus*, ed. Alexander Roberts, James Donaldson, and A. Cleveland Coxe, vol. 1, The Ante-Nicene Fathers (Buffalo, NY: Christian Literature Company, 1885), 330.

Maker, He the Creator, who made those things by Himself, that is, through His Word and His Wisdom—heaven and earth, and the seas, and all things that are in them: He is just; He is good; He it is who formed man, who planted paradise, who made the world, who gave rise to the flood, who saved Noah; He is the God of Abraham, and the God of Isaac, and the God of Jacob, the God of the living: He it is whom the law proclaims, whom the prophets preach, whom Christ reveals, whom the apostles make known to us, and in whom the Church believes. He is the Father of our Lord Jesus Christ: through His Word, who is His Son, through Him He is revealed and manifested to all to whom He *is* revealed; for those [only] know Him to whom the Son has revealed Him. But the Son, eternally co-existing with the Father, from of old, yea, from the beginning, always reveals the Father to Angels, Archangels, Powers, Virtues, and all to whom He wills that God should be revealed.[33]"

---

[33] Irenaeus of Lyons, "Irenæus against Heresies," in *The Apostolic Fathers with Justin Martyr and Irenaeus*, ed. Alexander Roberts, James Donaldson, and A. Cleveland Coxe, vol. 1, The Ante-Nicene Fathers (Buffalo, NY: Christian Literature Company, 1885), 406.

Once again Irenaeus plainly confesses faith in only one God.

- "1. We have learned from none others the plan of our salvation, than from those through whom the Gospel has come down to us, which they did at one time proclaim in public, and, at a later period, by the will of God, handed down to us in the Scriptures, to be the ground and pillar of our faith. For it is unlawful to assert that they preached before they possessed "perfect knowledge," as some do even venture to say, boasting themselves as improvers of the apostles. For, after our Lord rose from the dead, [the apostles] were invested with power from on high when the Holy Spirit came down [upon them], were filled from all [His gifts], and had perfect knowledge: they departed to the ends of the earth, preaching the glad tidings of the good things [sent] from God to us, and proclaiming the peace of heaven to men, who indeed do all equally and individually possess the Gospel of God. Matthew also issued a written Gospel among the Hebrews in their own dialect, while Peter and Paul were preaching at Rome, and laying the foundations of the Church. After their departure, Mark, the disciple and interpreter of Peter, did also hand down to us in writing what had been preached by Peter. Luke also, the companion of Paul, recorded in a book the Gospel preached by him. Afterwards, John, the disciple of the Lord, who also had leaned upon His breast, did himself publish a Gospel during his residence at Ephesus in Asia. 2. These have all declared to us that there is one God, Creator of heaven and earth, announced by the law and the prophets; and one Christ, the Son of God. If any one do not agree to these truths, he despises the companions of the Lord; nay more, he despises Christ Himself the Lord; yea, he despises the Father also, and stands self-condemned, resisting and opposing his own salvation, as is the case with all heretics.[34]"

Irenaeus, following so closely upon the heels of the apostles, tells us they preached one God, yet distinguished between the Father and Son as persons, declaring one must honor the Son to honor the Father. Cf *John 5:21-24*

- Wherefore, as I have already stated, no other is named as God, or is called Lord, except Him who is God and Lord of all,

---

[34] Irenaeus of Lyons, "Irenæus against Heresies," in *The Apostolic Fathers with Justin Martyr and Irenaeus*, ed. Alexander Roberts, James Donaldson, and A. Cleveland Coxe, vol. 1, The Ante-Nicene Fathers (Buffalo, NY: Christian Literature Company, 1885), 414–415.

> who also said to Moses, "I AM THAT I AM. And thus shalt thou say to the children of Israel: He who is, hath sent me unto you;" and His Son Jesus Christ our Lord, who makes those that believe in His name the sons of God. And again, when the Son speaks to Moses, He says, "I am come down to deliver this people." For it is He who descended and ascended for the salvation of men. Therefore God has been declared through the Son, who is in the Father, and has the Father in Himself—He WHO IS, the Father bearing witness to the Son, and the Son announcing the Father.—As also Esaias says, "I too am witness," he declares, "saith the LORD God, and the Son whom I have chosen, that ye may know, and believe, and understand that I AM."[35]"

Irenaeus is quite explicit in confessing his faith in only one God.

- "This, therefore, having been clearly demonstrated here (and it shall yet be so

[35] Irenaeus of Lyons, "Irenæus against Heresies," in *The Apostolic Fathers with Justin Martyr and Irenaeus*, ed. Alexander Roberts, James Donaldson, and A. Cleveland Coxe, vol. 1, The Ante-Nicene Fathers (Buffalo, NY: Christian Literature Company, 1885), 419.

still more clearly), that neither the prophets, nor the apostles, nor the Lord Christ in His own person, did acknowledge any other Lord or God, but the God and Lord supreme: the prophets and the apostles confessing the Father and the Son; but naming no other as God, and confessing no other as Lord: and the Lord Himself handing down to His disciples, that He, the Father, is the only God and Lord, who alone is God and ruler of all;—it is incumbent on us to follow, if we are their disciples indeed, their testimonies to this effect. For Matthew the apostle—knowing, as one and the same God, Him who had given promise to Abraham, that He would make his seed as the stars of heaven, and Him who, by His Son Christ Jesus, has called us to the knowledge of Himself, from the worship of stones, so that those who were not a people were made a people, and she beloved who was not beloved—declares that John, when preparing the way for Christ, said to those who were boasting of their relationship [to Abraham] according to the flesh, but who had their mind tinged and stuffed with all manner of evil, preaching that repentance which should call them back from their evil doings, said, "O generation of vipers, who hath shown you to flee from the wrath to come? Bring forth therefore fruit meet for repentance. And think not to say within yourselves, We have Abraham [to our] father: for I say unto you, that God is able of these stones to raise up children unto Abraham." He preached to them, therefore, the repentance from wickedness, but he did not declare to them another God, besides Him who made the promise to Abraham; he, the forerunner of Christ, of whom Matthew again says, and Luke likewise, "For this is he that was spoken of from the Lord by the prophet, The voice of one crying in the wilderness, Prepare ye the way of the Lord, make straight the paths of our God. Every valley shall be filled, and every mountain and hill brought low; and the crooked shall be made straight, and the rough into smooth ways; and all flesh shall see the salvation of God."[5] There is therefore one and the same God, the Father of our Lord, who also promised, through the prophets, that He would send His forerunner; and His salvation—that is, His Word—He caused to be made visible to all flesh, [the Word] Himself being made incarnate, that in all things their King might become manifest. For it is necessary that those [beings] which are judged do see the judge, and know Him from whom they receive judgment; and it is also proper, that those

> which follow on to glory should know Him who bestows upon them the gift of glory.[36]"

Irenaeus once again plainly yet eloquently sets forth his belief that there is only one God.

- "Such, then, are the first principles of the Gospel: that there is one God, the Maker of this universe; He who was also announced by the prophets, and who by Moses set forth the dispensation of the law,—[principles] which proclaim the Father of our Lord Jesus Christ, and ignore any other God or Father except Him.[37]"

---

[36] Irenaeus of Lyons, "Irenæus against Heresies," in *The Apostolic Fathers with Justin Martyr and Irenaeus*, ed. Alexander Roberts, James Donaldson, and A. Cleveland Coxe, vol. 1, The Ante-Nicene Fathers (Buffalo, NY: Christian Literature Company, 1885), 422.

[37] Irenaeus of Lyons, "Irenæus against Heresies," in *The Apostolic Fathers with Justin Martyr and Irenaeus*, ed. Alexander Roberts, James Donaldson, and A. Cleveland Coxe, vol. 1, The Ante-Nicene Fathers (Buffalo, NY: Christian Literature Company, 1885), 428.

Not only did Irenaeus confess faith in only one God, but also stated the prophets ignored any other god.

- "Again, our Lord Jesus Christ confesses this same Being as His Father, where He says: "I confess to thee, O Father, Lord of heaven and earth." What Father will those men have us to understand [by these words], those who are most perverse sophists of Pandora? Whether shall it be Bythus, whom they have fabled of themselves; or their Mother; or the Only-begotten? Or shall it be he whom the Marcionites or the others have invented as god (whom I indeed have amply demonstrated to be no god at all); or shall it be (what is really the case) the Maker of heaven and earth, whom also the prophets proclaimed,—whom Christ, too, confesses as His Father,—whom also the law announces, saying: "Hear, O Israel; The Lord thy God is one God?"[38]"

---

[38] Irenaeus of Lyons, "Irenæus against Heresies," in *The Apostolic Fathers with Justin Martyr and Irenaeus*, ed. Alexander Roberts, James Donaldson, and A. Cleveland Coxe, vol. 1, The Ante-Nicene Fathers (Buffalo, NY: Christian Literature Company, 1885), 463–464.

Irenaeus contends with heretics and affirms his belief in the one true God and Father or the Lord Jesus Christ.

- Wherefore, then, in all things, and through all things, there is one God, the Father, and one Word, and one Son, and one Spirit, and one salvation to all who believe in Him.[39]"

Here Irenaeus explicitly states his faith in one God.

- "Truly, then, the Scripture declared, which says, "First of all believe that there is one God, who has established all things, and completed them, and having caused that from what had no being, all things should come into existence:" He who contains all things, and is Himself contained by no one. Rightly also has Malachi said among the prophets: "Is it not one God who hath established us?

---

[39] Irenaeus of Lyons, "Irenæus against Heresies," in *The Apostolic Fathers with Justin Martyr and Irenaeus*, ed. Alexander Roberts, James Donaldson, and A. Cleveland Coxe, vol. 1, The Ante-Nicene Fathers (Buffalo, NY: Christian Literature Company, 1885), 469.

> Have we not all one Father?" In accordance with this, too, does the apostle say, "There is one God, the Father, who is above all, and in us all."[40]

Once again, we find Irenaeus' monotheistic confession.

- But as He who worketh all things in all is God, [as to the points] of what nature and how great He is, [God] is invisible and indescribable to all things which have been made by Him, but He is by no means unknown: for all things learn through His Word that there is one God the Father, who contains all things, and who grants existence to all, as is written in the Gospel: "No man hath seen God at any time, except the only-begotten Son,

---

[40] Irenaeus of Lyons, "Irenæus against Heresies," in *The Apostolic Fathers with Justin Martyr and Irenaeus*, ed. Alexander Roberts, James Donaldson, and A. Cleveland Coxe, vol. 1, The Ante-Nicene Fathers (Buffalo, NY: Christian Literature Company, 1885), 488.

who is in the bosom of the Father; He has declared [Him.]"[41]"

Once again, we find Irenaeus confessing his faith in one God.

- "But it is one and the same God, the Father of our Lord, from whom also the prophets had their mission, who does indeed, through His infinite kindness, call the unworthy; but He examines those who are called, [to ascertain] if they have on the garment fit and proper for the marriage of His Son, because nothing unbecoming or evil pleases Him. This is in accordance with what the Lord said to the man who had been healed: "Behold, thou art made whole; sin no more, lest a worse thing come unto thee." For he who is good, and righteous, and pure, and spotless, will endure nothing evil, nor unjust, nor detestable in His wedding chamber. This is the Father of our Lord, by whose providence all things consist, and all are administered by His command;

---

[41] Irenaeus of Lyons, "Irenæus against Heresies," in *The Apostolic Fathers with Justin Martyr and Irenaeus*, ed. Alexander Roberts, James Donaldson, and A. Cleveland Coxe, vol. 1, The Ante-Nicene Fathers (Buffalo, NY: Christian Literature Company, 1885), 489.

> and He confers His free gifts upon those who should [receive them]; but the most righteous Retributor metes out [punishment] according to their deserts, most deservedly, to the ungrateful and to those that are insensible of His kindness; and therefore does He say, "He sent His armies, and destroyed those murderers, and burned up their city."[42]"

Here Irenaeus confesses the one God is the Father of the Lord Jesus Christ and the God who sent the prophets of old. He also affirms this one God as our creator and judge of all.

- He thus plainly points out to those willing to hear, that is, to those having ears, that there is one God, the Father over all, and one Word of God, who is through all, by whom all things have been made; and that this world belongs to Him, and was made by Him, according to the Father's will, and not by angels; nor by apostasy, defect, and ignorance; nor by any power of Prunicus, whom certain of them also

---

[42] Irenaeus of Lyons, "Irenæus against Heresies," in *The Apostolic Fathers with Justin Martyr and Irenaeus*, ed. Alexander Roberts, James Donaldson, and A. Cleveland Coxe, vol. 1, The Ante-Nicene Fathers (Buffalo, NY: Christian Literature Company, 1885), 517.

call "the Mother;" nor by any other maker of the world ignorant of the Father.[43]"

Here is another of a multitude of statements affirming the ancient Christians believed in only one God.

- "Thus then does the Lord plainly show that it was the true Lord and the one God who had been set forth by the law; for Him whom the law proclaimed as God, the same did Christ point out as the Father, whom also it behoves the disciples of Christ alone to serve. [44]"

Irenaeus also affirmed that Jesus preached there is only one God, who has been set forth in the law, i.e., the Old Testament Scriptures.

---

[43] Irenaeus of Lyons, "Irenæus against Heresies," in *The Apostolic Fathers with Justin Martyr and Irenaeus*, ed. Alexander Roberts, James Donaldson, and A. Cleveland Coxe, vol. 1, The Ante-Nicene Fathers (Buffalo, NY: Christian Literature Company, 1885), 546.

[44] Irenaeus of Lyons, "Irenæus against Heresies," in *The Apostolic Fathers with Justin Martyr and Irenaeus*, ed. Alexander Roberts, James Donaldson, and A. Cleveland Coxe, vol. 1, The Ante-Nicene Fathers (Buffalo, NY: Christian Literature Company, 1885), 550.

- "there is one and the same God the Father, who was declared by the prophets, but made manifest by Christ.[45]"

Hardly a more explicitly monotheistic confession could ever have been made.

- "That we are not atheists, therefore, seeing that we acknowledge one God, uncreated, eternal, invisible, impassible, incomprehensible, illimitable, who is apprehended by the understanding only and the reason, who is encompassed by light, and beauty, and spirit, and power ineffable, by whom the universe has been created through His Logos, and set in order, and is kept in being—I have sufficiently demonstrated. [I say "His Logos"], for we acknowledge also a Son

---

[45] Irenaeus of Lyons, "Irenæus against Heresies," in *The Apostolic Fathers with Justin Martyr and Irenaeus*, ed. Alexander Roberts, James Donaldson, and A. Cleveland Coxe, vol. 1, The Ante-Nicene Fathers (Buffalo, NY: Christian Literature Company, 1885), 554.

of God. Nor let any one think it ridiculous that God should have a Son."[46]

Theophilus of Antioch, AD115-181, lived and ministered in Antioch, Syria, the same place from which Paul and Barnabas were sent. He, too, confesses the monotheistic faith.

- "This Jesus, who is eternal, the one great High Priest of the one God and of His Father, prays for and exhorts men."[47]

---

[46] Theophilus of Antioch, "Theophilus to Autolycus," in *Fathers of the Second Century: Hermas, Tatian, Athenagoras, Theophilus, and Clement of Alexandria (Entire)*, ed. Alexander Roberts, James Donaldson, and A. Cleveland Coxe, trans. Marcus Dods, vol. 2, The Ante-Nicene Fathers (Buffalo, NY: Christian Literature Company, 1885), 103.

[47] Clement of Alexandria, "Exhortation to the Heathen," in *Fathers of the Second Century: Hermas, Tatian, Athenagoras, Theophilus, and Clement of Alexandria (Entire)*, ed. Alexander Roberts, James Donaldson, and A. Cleveland

Clement of Alexandria, AD153-217, is among the latest of writers we will consider. Alexandria was by no means a bastion of conservative orthodoxy, yet this confession demonstrates the historical reality of the continued belief in only one God.

- "So that it is veritably clear that the God of all is only one good, just Creator, and the Son in the Father, to whom be glory for ever and ever, Amen. [48]"
- ""Now the just shall live by faith," which is according to the covenant and the commandments; since these, which are two in name and time, given in accordance with the [divine] economy—being in power one—the old and the new,

---

Coxe, vol. 2, The Ante-Nicene Fathers (Buffalo, NY: Christian Literature Company, 1885), 205–206.

[48] Clement of Alexandria, "The Instructor," in *Fathers of the Second Century: Hermas, Tatian, Athenagoras, Theophilus, and Clement of Alexandria (Entire)*, ed. Alexander Roberts, James Donaldson, and A. Cleveland Coxe, vol. 2, The Ante-Nicene Fathers (Buffalo, NY: Christian Literature Company, 1885), 228.

are dispensed through the Son by one God.[49]"

Though the multitude of texts is a bit wearisome, we continue for the purpose of demonstrating the 1st-2nd century belief in the one true God.

- "Wherefore also the apostle designates as "the express image (χαρακτῆρα) of the glory of the Father" the Son, who taught the truth respecting God, and expressed the fact that the Almighty is the one and only God and Father, "whom no man knoweth but the Son, and he to whom the Son shall reveal Him." That God is one is intimated by those "who seek the face of the God of Jacob;" whom being the only God, our Saviour and God characterizes as the Good Father. And "the generation of those that seek Him" is the elect race, devoted to inquiry after knowledge. Wherefore also the apostle says, "I shall

---

[49] Clement of Alexandria, "The Stromata, or Miscellanies," in *Fathers of the Second Century: Hermas, Tatian, Athenagoras, Theophilus, and Clement of Alexandria (Entire)*, ed. Alexander Roberts, James Donaldson, and A. Cleveland Coxe, vol. 2, The Ante-Nicene Fathers (Buffalo, NY: Christian Literature Company, 1885), 354.

profit you nothing, unless I speak to you, either by revelation, or by knowledge, or by prophecy, or by doctrine."[50]"

Clement again confesses the monotheistic character of the Christian faith.

The Ante-Nicene Fathers Believed the Father, Son, And the Holy Spirit Are Distinct Persons in The One True God.

- "They did not nail him then, but simply bound him. And he, placing his hands behind him, and being bound like a distinguished ram [taken] out of a great flock for sacrifice, and prepared to be an acceptable burnt-offering unto God, looked up to heaven, and said, "O Lord God Almighty, the Father of thy beloved and blessed Son Jesus Christ, by whom we have received the knowledge of Thee, the God of angels and powers, and of every creature, and of the whole race of

---

[50] Clement of Alexandria, "The Stromata, or Miscellanies," in *Fathers of the Second Century: Hermas, Tatian, Athenagoras, Theophilus, and Clement of Alexandria (Entire)*, ed. Alexander Roberts, James Donaldson, and A. Cleveland Coxe, vol. 2, The Ante-Nicene Fathers (Buffalo, NY: Christian Literature Company, 1885), 539.

> the righteous who live before thee, I give Thee thanks that Thou hast counted me worthy of this day and this hour, that I should have a part in the number of Thy martyrs, in the cup of thy Christ, to the resurrection of eternal life, both of soul and body, through the incorruption [imparted] by the Holy Ghost. Among whom may I be accepted this day before Thee as a fat and acceptable sacrifice, according as Thou, the ever-truthful[5] God, hast fore-ordained, hast revealed beforehand to me, and now hast fulfilled. Wherefore also I praise Thee for all things, I bless Thee, I glorify Thee, along with the everlasting and heavenly Jesus Christ, Thy beloved Son, with whom, to Thee, and the Holy Ghost, be glory both now and to all coming ages. Amen."[51]"
> [A.D. 65–100–155.]

This prayer of Polycarp is plainly Trinitarian in nature, as he confesses Father, Son, and Holy Spirit as distinct persons in the Godhead.

---

[51] Alexander Roberts, James Donaldson, and A. Cleveland Coxe, eds., "The Encyclical Epistle of the Church at Smyrna," in *The Apostolic Fathers with Justin Martyr and Irenaeus*, vol. 1, The Ante-Nicene Fathers (Buffalo, NY: Christian Literature Company, 1885), 42.

- “But our Physician is the only true God, the unbegotten and unapproachable, the Lord of all, the Father and Begetter of the only-begotten Son. We have also as a Physician the Lord our God, Jesus the Christ, the only-begotten Son and Word, before time began, but who afterwards became also man, of Mary the virgin. For “the Word was made flesh.”[11] Being incorporeal, He was in the body; being impassible, He was in a passible body; being immortal, He was in a mortal body; being life, He became subject to corruption, that He might free our souls from death and corruption, and heal them, and might restore them to health, when they were diseased with ungodliness and wicked lusts.[52]” [A.D. 30–107.]

Notice how Ignatius speaks of Jesus as being the Word (John 1:1) and only begotten (John 1:14,18), and as being eternal. He obviously distinguishes between the Father and the Son while maintaining their essential unity in essence.

---

[52] Ignatius of Antioch, “The Epistle of Ignatius to the Ephesians,” in *The Apostolic Fathers with Justin Martyr and Irenaeus*, ed. Alexander Roberts, James Donaldson, and A. Cleveland Coxe, vol. 1, The Ante-Nicene Fathers (Buffalo, NY: Christian Literature Company, 1885), 52.

- "Our Lord and God, Jesus Christ, the Son of the living God[53]"

Notice how Ignatius here speaks of Jesus as Lord, God, and the Son of God. He is both God and the Son of God, thus showing Ignatius believed there was one God and yet a distinction was to be seen between the Son and God (the Father).

- "For the Son of God, who was begotten before time began, and established all things according to the will of the Father[54]"

Again, we see Ignatius distinguish between the Father and the Son. He also speaks of the Son as being Son before time, that is, eternally. His confession is that

[53] Ignatius of Antioch, "The Epistle of Ignatius to the Ephesians," in *The Apostolic Fathers with Justin Martyr and Irenaeus*, ed. Alexander Roberts, James Donaldson, and A. Cleveland Coxe, vol. 1, The Ante-Nicene Fathers (Buffalo, NY: Christian Literature Company, 1885), 56.

[54] Ignatius of Antioch, "The Epistle of Ignatius to the Ephesians," in *The Apostolic Fathers with Justin Martyr and Irenaeus*, ed. Alexander Roberts, James Donaldson, and A. Cleveland Coxe, vol. 1, The Ante-Nicene Fathers (Buffalo, NY: Christian Literature Company, 1885), 57.

the Son has always been uniquely the Son. Fathers and sons are persons and not mere manifestations or titles.

- "For they alienate Christ from the Father, and the law from Christ. They also calumniate His being born of the Virgin; they are ashamed of His cross; they deny His passion; and they do not believe His resurrection. They introduce God as a Being unknown; they suppose Christ to be unbegotten; and as to the Spirit, they do not admit that He exists. Some of them say that the Son is a mere man, and that the Father, Son, and Holy Spirit are but the same person, and that the creation is the work of God, not by Christ, but by some other strange power.[55]"

Notice Ignatius' stance that the Father, Son, and Holy Spirit are not to be considered the same person. This is Trinitarian doctrine, even if he does not use the term.

---

[55] Ignatius of Antioch, "The Epistle of Ignatius to the Trallians," in *The Apostolic Fathers with Justin Martyr and Irenaeus*, ed. Alexander Roberts, James Donaldson, and A. Cleveland Coxe, vol. 1, The Ante-Nicene Fathers (Buffalo, NY: Christian Literature Company, 1885), 68.

- "Ignatius, who is also called Theophorus, to the Church which has obtained mercy, through the majesty of the Most High God the Father, and of Jesus Christ, His only-begotten Son; the Church which is sanctified and enlightened by the will of God, who formed all things that are according to the faith and love of Jesus Christ, our God and Saviour; the Church which presides in the place of the region of the Romans, and which is worthy of God, worthy of honour, worthy of the highest happiness, worthy of praise, worthy of credit, worthy of being deemed holy, and which presides over love, is named from Christ, and from the Father, and is possessed of the Spirit, which I also salute in the name of Almighty God, and of Jesus Christ His Son: to those who are united, both according to the flesh and spirit, to every one of His commandments, who are filled inseparably with all the grace of God, and are purified from every strange taint, [I wish] abundance of happiness unblameably, in God, even the Father, and our Lord Jesus Christ.[56]"

---

[56] Ignatius of Antioch, "The Epistle of Ignatius to the Romans," in *The Apostolic Fathers with Justin Martyr and Irenaeus*, ed. Alexander Roberts, James Donaldson,

Ignatius' Trinitarian faith is plainly presented in this statement.

- "Since, also, there is but one unbegotten Being, God, even the Father; and one only-begotten Son, God, the Word and man; and one Comforter, the Spirit of truth; and also one preaching, and one faith, and one baptism; and one Church which the holy apostles established from one end of the earth to the other by the blood of Christ, and by their own sweat and toil; it behoves you also, therefore, as "a peculiar people, and a holy nation,"[3] to perform all things with harmony in Christ.[57]"

Again, long before the Roman Catholic Church and papacy which began in the fifth century, this explicit

---

and A. Cleveland Coxe, vol. 1, The Ante-Nicene Fathers (Buffalo, NY: Christian Literature Company, 1885), 73.

[57] Ignatius of Antioch, "The Epistle of Ignatius to the Philadelphians," in *The Apostolic Fathers with Justin Martyr and Irenaeus*, ed. Alexander Roberts, James Donaldson, and A. Cleveland Coxe, vol. 1, The Ante-Nicene Fathers (Buffalo, NY: Christian Literature Company, 1885), 81.

confession was written of one God who is distinctly revealed as three Divine Persons.

- "If any one preaches the one God of the law and the prophets, but denies Christ to be the Son of God, he is a liar, even as also is his father the devil, and is a Jew falsely so called, being possessed of[6] mere carnal circumcision. If any one confesses Christ Jesus the Lord, but denies the God of the law and of the prophets, saying that the Father of Christ is not the Maker of heaven and earth, he has not continued in the truth any more than his father the devil, and is a disciple of Simon Magus, not of the Holy Spirit. If any one says there is one God, and also confesses Christ Jesus, but thinks the Lord to be a mere man, and not the only-begotten God, and Wisdom, and the Word of God, and deems Him to consist merely of a soul and body, such an one is a serpent, that preaches deceit and error for the destruction of men. And such a man is poor in understanding, even as by name he is an Ebionite.[9] If any one confesses the truths mentioned, but calls lawful wedlock, and the procreation of children, destruction and pollution, or deems certain kinds of food abominable, such an one has the apostate dragon dwelling

> within him. If any one confesses the Father, and the Son, and the Holy Ghost, and praises the creation, but calls the incarnation merely an appearance, and is ashamed of the passion, such an one has denied the faith, not less than the Jews who killed Christ. If any one confesses these things, and that God the Word did dwell in a human body, being within it as the Word, even as the soul also is in the body, because it was God that inhabited it, and not a human soul, but affirms that unlawful unions are a good thing, and places the highest happiness in pleasure, as does the man who is falsely called a Nicolaitan, this person can neither be a lover of God, nor a lover of Christ, but is a corrupter of his own flesh, and therefore void of the Holy Spirit, and a stranger to Christ. [58]"

Ignatius was contending with the Christological heresies of the Gnostics and, as he did so, presents to us his faith in the Trinitarian nature of God by speaking of one God and Christ the only begotten God, which shows

---

[58] Ignatius of Antioch, "The Epistle of Ignatius to the Philadelphians," in *The Apostolic Fathers with Justin Martyr and Irenaeus*, ed. Alexander Roberts, James Donaldson, and A. Cleveland Coxe, vol. 1, The Ante-Nicene Fathers (Buffalo, NY: Christian Literature Company, 1885), 83.

us both the unity of God as well as the distinction between Father and Son.

- "I GLORIFY the God and Father of our Lord Jesus Christ, who by Him has given you such wisdom. For I have observed that ye are perfected in an immoveable faith, as if ye were nailed to the cross of our Lord Jesus Christ, both in the flesh and in the spirit, and are established in love through the blood of Christ, being fully persuaded, in very truth, with respect to our Lord Jesus Christ, that He was the Son of God, "the first-born of every creature," God the Word, the only-begotten Son, and was of the seed of David according to the flesh, by the Virgin Mary; was baptized by John, that all righteousness might be fulfilled[10] by Him; that He lived a life of holiness without sin, and was truly, under Pontius Pilate and Herod the tetrarch, nailed [to the cross] for us in His flesh. From whom we also derive our being, from His divinely-blessed passion, that He might set up a standard for the ages, through His resurrection, to all His holy and faithful [followers], whether among Jews or

Gentiles, in the one body of His Church.[59]"

Can we find any more plainly Trinitarian confession than this, as the Deity and Personal distinctiveness of the Father and the Son are confessed?

- "What, again, says Moses to Jesus (Joshua) the son of Nave, when he gave him this name, as being a prophet, with this view only, that all the people might hear that the Father would reveal all things concerning His Son Jesus to the son of Nave? This name then being given him when he sent him to spy out the land, he said, "Take a book into thy hands, and write what the Lord declares, that the Son of God will in the last days cut off from the roots all the house of Amalek." Behold again: Jesus who was manifested, both by type and in the flesh, is not the Son of man, but the Son of God. Since, therefore, they were to say that Christ was

---

[59] Ignatius of Antioch, "The Epistle of Ignatius to the Smyrnæans," in *The Apostolic Fathers with Justin Martyr and Irenaeus*, ed. Alexander Roberts, James Donaldson, and A. Cleveland Coxe, vol. 1, The Ante-Nicene Fathers (Buffalo, NY: Christian Literature Company, 1885), 86.

> the son of David, fearing and understanding the error of the wicked, he saith, "The Lord said unto my Lord, Sit at My right hand, until I make Thine enemies Thy footstool."[17] And again, thus saith Isaiah, "The Lord said to Christ, my Lord, whose right hand I have holden,[19] that the nations should yield obedience before Him; and I will break in pieces the strength of kings." Behold how David calleth Him Lord and the Son of God.[60]"

Another passage speaking of the distinction between the Father and the Son.

- "...they ascend through the Spirit to the Son, and through the Son to the Father; and that in due time the Son will yield up His work to the Father, even as it is said by the apostle, "For He must reign till He hath put all enemies under His feet. The last enemy that shall be destroyed is death." For in the times of the kingdom the just man who is on the earth shall forget to die. "But when He saith all

[60] Alexander Roberts, James Donaldson, and A. Cleveland Coxe, eds., "The Epistle of Barnabas," in *The Apostolic Fathers with Justin Martyr and Irenaeus*, vol. 1, The Ante-Nicene Fathers (Buffalo, NY: Christian Literature Company, 1885), 145.

things are put under Him, it is manifest that He is excepted which did put all things under Him. And when all things shall be subdued unto Him, then shall the Son also Himself be subject unto Him that put all things under Him, that God may be all in all."[61]"

Papias is explicit in his faith in the personal distinction between the Persons of God, The Father, Son, and Holy Spirit.

- "That all these things should come to pass, I say, our Teacher foretold, He who is both Son and Apostle of God the Father of all and the Ruler, Jesus Christ; from whom also we have the name of Christians.[62]

[61] Papias, "Fragments of Papias," in *The Apostolic Fathers with Justin Martyr and Irenaeus*, ed. Alexander Roberts, James Donaldson, and A. Cleveland Coxe, vol. 1, The Ante-Nicene Fathers (Buffalo, NY: Christian Literature Company, 1885), 154.

[62] Justin Martyr, "The First Apology of Justin," in *The Apostolic Fathers with Justin Martyr and Irenaeus*, ed. Alexander Roberts, James Donaldson, and A. Cleveland Coxe, vol. 1, The Ante-Nicene Fathers (Buffalo, NY: Christian Literature Company, 1885), 166.

A very stark and plain distinction between the Son who was sent and the Father who sent Him.

- "Our teacher of these things is Jesus Christ, who also was born for this purpose, and was crucified under Pontius Pilate, procurator of Judæa, in the times of Tiberius Cæsar; and that we reasonably worship Him, having learned that He is the Son of the true God Himself, and holding Him in the second place, and the prophetic Spirit in the third, we will prove. For they proclaim our madness to consist in this, that we give to a crucified man a place second to the unchangeable and eternal God, the Creator of all; for they do not discern the mystery that is herein, to which, as we make it plain to you, we pray you to give heed.[63]"

Just as we speak of the Father, Son, and Holy Spirit as the first, second, and third persons of the Godhead/One true God, so Justin did; and he plainly

---

[63] Justin Martyr, "The First Apology of Justin," in *The Apostolic Fathers with Justin Martyr and Irenaeus*, ed. Alexander Roberts, James Donaldson, and A. Cleveland Coxe, vol. 1, The Ante-Nicene Fathers (Buffalo, NY: Christian Literature Company, 1885), 166–167.

declared Jesus was worshiped as God while being personally distinguished from the Father.

- He who spake to him was indeed the Son of God, who is called both Angel and Apostle, are justly charged, both by the Spirit of prophecy and by Christ Himself, with knowing neither the Father nor the Son. For they who affirm that the Son is the Father, are proved neither to have become acquainted with the Father, nor to know that the Father of the universe has a Son; who also, being the first-begotten Word of God, is even God. And of old He appeared in the shape of fire and in the likeness of an angel to Moses and to the other prophets; but now in the times of your reign, having, as we before said, become Man by a virgin, according to the counsel of the Father, for the salvation of those who believe on Him, He endured both to be set at nought and to suffer, that by dying and rising again He might conquer death. And that which was said out of the bush to Moses, "I am that I am, the God of Abraham, and the God of Isaac, and the God of Jacob, and the God of your fathers," this signified that they, even though dead, are yet in existence, and are men belonging to Christ Himself. For they were the first of all men to busy themselves in the search after God; Abraham being the father of Isaac, and Isaac of Jacob, as Moses wrote.[64]"

Notice, as Justin speaks of Christ, he declares the Father and the Son to both be God while distinct from each other. That is what Trinitarian doctrine affirms, the One True God is three distinct persons, Father, Son, and Holy Spirit.

- "And the same sentiment was expressed, my friends, by the word of God [written] by Moses, when it indicated to us, with regard to Him whom it has pointed out, that God speaks in the creation of man with the very same design, in the following words: 'Let Us make man after our image and likeness. And let them have dominion over the fish of the sea, and over the fowl of the heaven, and over the cattle, and over all the earth, and over all the creeping things that creep on the earth. And God created man: after the image of God did He create him; male

---

[64] Justin Martyr, "The First Apology of Justin," in *The Apostolic Fathers with Justin Martyr and Irenaeus*, ed. Alexander Roberts, James Donaldson, and A. Cleveland Coxe, vol. 1, The Ante-Nicene Fathers (Buffalo, NY: Christian Literature Company, 1885), 184.

and female created He them. And God blessed them, and said, Increase and multiply, and fill the earth, and have power over it.[4] And that you may not change the [force of the] words just quoted, and repeat what your teachers assert,—either that God said to Himself, 'Let Us make,' just as we, when about to do something, oftentimes say to ourselves, 'Let us make;' or that God spoke to the elements, to wit, the earth and other similar substances of which we believe man was formed, 'Let Us make,'—I shall quote again the words narrated by Moses himself, from which we can indisputably learn that [God] conversed with some one who was numerically distinct from Himself, and also a rational Being. These are the words: 'And God said, Behold, Adam has become as one of us, to know good and evil.' In saying, therefore, 'as one of us,' [Moses] has declared that [there is a certain] number of persons associated with one another, and that they are at least two. For I would not say that the dogma of that heresy which is said to be among you is true, or that the teachers of it can prove that [God] spoke to angels, or that the human frame was the workmanship of angels. But this Offspring, which was truly brought forth from the Father, was with the Father before all the creatures, and the Father communed with Him; even as the Scripture by Solomon has made clear, that He whom Solomon calls Wisdom, was begotten as a Beginning before all His creatures and as Offspring by God[65]"

Justin uses the "us" in the Creation Account to teach Christ as the eternal Son of God, Who was distinct from the Father while one with Him in being and essence.

- "For I have proved that it was Jesus who appeared to and conversed with Moses, and Abraham, and all the other patriarchs without exception, ministering to the will of the Father; who also, I say, came to be born man by the Virgin Mary, and lives for ever. For the latter is He after whom and by whom the Father will renew both the heaven and the earth; this is He who shall shine an eternal light in Jerusalem; this is he who is the king of Salem after

---

[65] Justin Martyr, "Dialogue of Justin with Trypho, a Jew," in *The Apostolic Fathers with Justin Martyr and Irenaeus*, ed. Alexander Roberts, James Donaldson, and A. Cleveland Coxe, vol. 1, The Ante-Nicene Fathers (Buffalo, NY: Christian Literature Company, 1885), 228.

> the order of Melchizedek, and the eternal Priest of the Most High. [66]

This is only rational if Justin believed there was a distinction between the Son and the Father who sent Him.

- "And others of them, with great craftiness, adapted such parts of Scripture to their own figments, lead away captive from the truth those who do not retain a stedfast faith in one God, the Father Almighty, and in one Lord Jesus Christ, the Son of God.[67]"

Unless the Father can be His own Son, this again plainly shows the personal distinction between the two.

---

[66] Justin Martyr, "Dialogue of Justin with Trypho, a Jew," in *The Apostolic Fathers with Justin Martyr and Irenaeus*, ed. Alexander Roberts, James Donaldson, and A. Cleveland Coxe, vol. 1, The Ante-Nicene Fathers (Buffalo, NY: Christian Literature Company, 1885), 255.

[67] Irenaeus of Lyons, "Irenæus against Heresies," in *The Apostolic Fathers with Justin Martyr and Irenaeus*, ed. Alexander Roberts, James Donaldson, and A. Cleveland Coxe, vol. 1, The Ante-Nicene Fathers (Buffalo, NY: Christian Literature Company, 1885), 320.

- "The Church, though dispersed throughout the whole world, even to the ends of the earth, has received from the apostles and their disciples this faith: [She believes] in one God, the Father Almighty, Maker of heaven, and earth, and the sea, and all things that are in them; and in one Christ Jesus, the Son of God, who became incarnate for our salvation; and in the Holy Spirit, who proclaimed through the prophets the dispensations of God, and the advents, and the birth from a virgin, and the passion, and the resurrection from the dead, and the ascension into heaven in the flesh of the beloved Christ Jesus, our Lord, and His [future] manifestation from heaven in the glory of the Father "to gather all things in one," and to raise up anew all flesh of the whole human race, in order that to Christ Jesus, our Lord, and God, and Saviour, and King, according to the will of the invisible Father, "every knee should bow, of things in heaven, and things in earth, and things under the earth, and that every tongue should confess" to Him[68]" "As I have already observed, the

---

[68] Irenaeus of Lyons, "Irenæus against Heresies," in *The Apostolic Fathers with Justin Martyr and Irenaeus*, ed. Alexander Roberts, James Donaldson, and A. Cleveland

Church, having received this preaching and this faith, although scattered throughout the whole world, yet, as if occupying but one house, carefully preserves it. She also believes these points [of doctrine] just as if she had but one soul, and one and the same heart, and she proclaims them, and teaches them, and hands them down, with perfect harmony, as if she possessed only one mouth. For, although the languages of the world are dissimilar, yet the import of the tradition is one and the same. For the Churches which have been planted in Germany do not believe or hand down anything different, nor do those in Spain, nor those in Gaul, nor those in the East, nor those in Egypt, nor those in Libya, nor those which have been established in the central regions of the world. But as the sun, that creature of God, is one and the same throughout the whole world, so also the preaching of the truth shineth everywhere, and enlightens all men that are willing to come to a knowledge of the truth. Nor will any one of the rulers in the Churches, however highly gifted he may be in point of eloquence, teach doctrines different

---

Coxe, vol. 1, The Ante-Nicene Fathers (Buffalo, NY: Christian Literature Company, 1885), 330.

from these (for no one is greater than the Master); nor, on the other hand, will he who is deficient in power of expression inflict injury on the tradition. For the faith being ever one and the same, neither does one who is able at great length to discourse regarding it, make any addition to it, nor does one, who can say but little diminish it.[69]"

This is an amazingly plain presentation of Trinitarian theology.

- "But there is one only God, the Creator—He who is above every Principality, and Power, and Dominion, and Virtue: He is Father, He is God, He the Founder, He the Maker, He the Creator, who made those things by Himself, that is, through His Word and His Wisdom—heaven and earth, and the seas, and all things that are in them: He is just; He is good; He it is who formed man, who planted paradise, who made the world, who gave rise to the flood, who saved Noah; He is the God of

---

[69] Irenaeus of Lyons, "Irenæus against Heresies," in *The Apostolic Fathers with Justin Martyr and Irenaeus*, ed. Alexander Roberts, James Donaldson, and A. Cleveland Coxe, vol. 1, The Ante-Nicene Fathers (Buffalo, NY: Christian Literature Company, 1885), 331.

> Abraham, and the God of Isaac, and the God of Jacob, the God of the living: He it is whom the law proclaims, whom the prophets preach, whom Christ reveals, whom the apostles make known to us, and in whom the Church believes. He is the Father of our Lord Jesus Christ: through His Word, who is His Son, through Him He is revealed and manifested to all to whom He *is* revealed; for those [only] know Him to whom the Son has revealed Him. But the Son, eternally co-existing with the Father, from of old, yea, from the beginning, always reveals the Father to Angels, Archangels, Powers, Virtues, and all to whom He wills that God should be revealed.[70]"

Here Irenaeus shows the belief in one God while maintaining the eternal existence of the Son as a person distinct yet not separate from the Father.

- "1. We have learned from none others the plan of our salvation, than from those through whom the Gospel has come down

---

[70] Irenaeus of Lyons, "Irenæus against Heresies," in *The Apostolic Fathers with Justin Martyr and Irenaeus*, ed. Alexander Roberts, James Donaldson, and A. Cleveland Coxe, vol. 1, The Ante-Nicene Fathers (Buffalo, NY: Christian Literature Company, 1885), 406.

to us, which they did at one time proclaim in public, and, at a later period, by the will of God, handed down to us in the Scriptures, to be the ground and pillar of our faith. For it is unlawful to assert that they preached before they possessed "perfect knowledge," as some do even venture to say, boasting themselves as improvers of the apostles. For, after our Lord rose from the dead, [the apostles] were invested with power from on high when the Holy Spirit came down [upon them], were filled from all [His gifts], and had perfect knowledge: they departed to the ends of the earth, preaching the glad tidings of the good things [sent] from God to us, and proclaiming the peace of heaven to men, who indeed do all equally and individually possess the Gospel of God. Matthew also issued a written Gospel among the Hebrews in their own dialect, while Peter and Paul were preaching at Rome, and laying the foundations of the Church. After their departure, Mark, the disciple and interpreter of Peter, did also hand down to us in writing what had been preached by Peter. Luke also, the companion of Paul, recorded in a book the Gospel preached by him. Afterwards, John, the disciple of the Lord, who also had leaned upon His breast, did himself publish a Gospel during his residence at Ephesus in Asia. 2. These have all declared to us that there is one God, Creator of heaven and earth, announced by the law and the prophets; and one Christ, the Son of God. If any one do not agree to these truths, he despises the companions of the Lord; nay more, he despises Christ Himself the Lord; yea, he despises the Father also, and stands self-condemned, resisting and opposing his own salvation, as is the case with all heretics.[71]"

Irenaeus, following so closely upon the heels of the apostles, tells us they preached one God, yet distinguished between the Father and Son as persons, declaring one must honor the Son to honor the Father. Cf *John 5:21-24*

- "This is also made clear from the words of the Lord, who did truly reveal the Son of God to those of the circumcision—Him who had been foretold as Christ by the prophets; that is, He set Himself forth, who had restored liberty to men, and

---

[71] Irenaeus of Lyons, "Irenæus against Heresies," in *The Apostolic Fathers with Justin Martyr and Irenaeus*, ed. Alexander Roberts, James Donaldson, and A. Cleveland Coxe, vol. 1, The Ante-Nicene Fathers (Buffalo, NY: Christian Literature Company, 1885), 414–415.

> bestowed on them the inheritance of incorruption. And again, the apostles taught the Gentiles that they should leave vain stocks and stones, which they imagined to be gods, and worship the true God, who had created and made all the human family, and, by means of His creation, did nourish, increase, strengthen, and preserve them in being; and that they might look for His Son Jesus Christ, who redeemed us from apostasy with His own blood, so that we should also be a sanctified people,—who shall also descend from heaven in His Father's power, and pass judgment upon all, and who shall freely give the good things of God to those who shall have kept His commandments.[72]"

Again, the personal distinction between the Father and the Son is presented here as being apostolic doctrine in the early church long before Roman Catholicism came into being.

---

[72] Irenaeus of Lyons, "Irenæus against Heresies," in *The Apostolic Fathers with Justin Martyr and Irenaeus*, ed. Alexander Roberts, James Donaldson, and A. Cleveland Coxe, vol. 1, The Ante-Nicene Fathers (Buffalo, NY: Christian Literature Company, 1885), 418.

- "Therefore neither would the Lord, nor the Holy Spirit, nor the apostles, have ever named as God, definitely and absolutely, him who was not God, unless he were truly God; nor would they have named any one in his own person Lord, except God the Father ruling over all, and His Son who has received dominion from His Father over all creation, as this passage has it: "The LORD said unto my Lord, Sit Thou at my right hand, until I make Thine enemies Thy footstool." Here the [Scripture] represents to us the Father addressing the Son; He who gave Him the inheritance of the heathen, and subjected to Him all His enemies. Since, therefore, the Father is truly Lord, and the Son truly Lord, the Holy Spirit has fitly designated them by the title of Lord. And again, referring to the destruction of the Sodomites, the Scripture says, "Then the LORD rained upon Sodom and upon Gomorrah fire and brimstone from the LORD out of heaven." For it here points out that the Son, who had also been talking with Abraham, had received power to judge the Sodomites for their wickedness. And this [text following] does declare the same truth: "Thy throne, O God, is for ever and ever; the sceptre of Thy kingdom is a right sceptre. Thou hast loved righteousness, and hated iniquity:

therefore God, Thy God, hath anointed Thee." For the Spirit designates both [of them] by the name, of God—both Him who is anointed as Son, and Him who does anoint, that is, the Father. And again: "God stood in the congregation of the gods, He judges among the gods." He [here] refers to the Father and the Son, and those who have received the adoption; but these are the Church. For she is the synagogue of God, which God—that is, the Son Himself—has gathered by Himself. Of whom He again speaks: "The God of gods, the Lord hath spoken, and hath called the earth." Who is meant by God? He of whom He has said, "God shall come openly, our God, and shall not keep silence;"[4] that is, the Son, who came manifested to men who said, "I have openly appeared to those who seek Me not." But of what gods [does he speak]? [Of those] to whom He says, "I have said, Ye are gods, and all sons of the Most High." To those, no doubt, who have received the grace of the "adoption, by which we cry, Abba Father."[73]""

---

[73] Irenaeus of Lyons, "Irenæus against Heresies," in *The Apostolic Fathers with Justin Martyr and Irenaeus*, ed. Alexander Roberts, James Donaldson, and A. Cleveland

> Wherefore, as I have already stated, no other is named as God, or is called Lord, except Him who is God and Lord of all, who also said to Moses, "I AM THAT I AM. And thus shalt thou say to the children of Israel: He who is, hath sent me unto you;" and His Son Jesus Christ our Lord, who makes those that believe in His name the sons of God. And again, when the Son speaks to Moses, He says, "I am come down to deliver this people." For it is He who descended and ascended for the salvation of men. Therefore God has been declared through the Son, who is in the Father, and has the Father in Himself—He WHO IS, the Father bearing witness to the Son, and the Son announcing the Father.—As also Esaias says, "I too am witness," he declares, "saith the LORD God, and the Son whom I have chosen, that ye may know, and believe, and understand that I AM."[74]"

Coxe, vol. 1, The Ante-Nicene Fathers (Buffalo, NY: Christian Literature Company, 1885), 418–419.

[74] Irenaeus of Lyons, "Irenæus against Heresies," in *The Apostolic Fathers with Justin Martyr and Irenaeus*, ed. Alexander Roberts, James Donaldson, and A. Cleveland Coxe, vol. 1, The Ante-Nicene Fathers (Buffalo, NY: Christian Literature Company, 1885), 419.

Irenaeus insists upon the essential Deity of both the Father and the Son, while maintaining faith in their personal distinction.

- "Wherefore I do also call upon thee, LORD God of Abraham, and God of Isaac, and God of Jacob and Israel, who art the Father of our Lord Jesus Christ, the God who, through the abundance of Thy mercy, hast had a favour towards us, that we should know Thee, who hast made heaven and earth, who rulest over all, who art the only and the true God, above whom there is none other God; grant, by our Lord Jesus Christ, the governing power of the Holy Spirit; give to every reader of this book to know Thee, that Thou art God alone, to be strengthened in Thee, and to avoid every heretical, and godless, and impious doctrine.[75]"

A Trinitarian prayer from Irenaeus.

---

[75] Irenaeus of Lyons, "Irenæus against Heresies," in *The Apostolic Fathers with Justin Martyr and Irenaeus*, ed. Alexander Roberts, James Donaldson, and A. Cleveland Coxe, vol. 1, The Ante-Nicene Fathers (Buffalo, NY: Christian Literature Company, 1885), 419.

- "This, therefore, having been clearly demonstrated here (and it shall yet be so still more clearly), that neither the prophets, nor the apostles, nor the Lord Christ in His own person, did acknowledge any other Lord or God, but the God and Lord supreme: the prophets and the apostles confessing the Father and the Son; but naming no other as God, and confessing no other as Lord: and the Lord Himself handing down to His disciples, that He, the Father, is the only God and Lord, who alone is God and ruler of all;—it is incumbent on us to follow, if we are their disciples indeed, their testimonies to this effect. For Matthew the apostle—knowing, as one and the same God, Him who had given promise to Abraham, that He would make his seed as the stars of heaven, and Him who, by His Son Christ Jesus, has called us to the knowledge of Himself, from the worship of stones, so that those who were not a people were made a people, and she beloved who was not beloved—declares that John, when preparing the way for Christ, said to those who were boasting of their relationship [to Abraham] according to the flesh, but who had their mind tinged and stuffed with all manner of evil, preaching that repentance which should call them back from their evil doings, said, "O generation of vipers, who hath shown you to flee from the wrath to come? Bring forth therefore fruit meet for repentance. And think not to say within yourselves, We have Abraham [to our] father: for I say unto you, that God is able of these stones to raise up children unto Abraham." He preached to them, therefore, the repentance from wickedness, but he did not declare to them another God, besides Him who made the promise to Abraham; he, the forerunner of Christ, of whom Matthew again says, and Luke likewise, "For this is he that was spoken of from the Lord by the prophet, The voice of one crying in the wilderness, Prepare ye the way of the Lord, make straight the paths of our God. Every valley shall be filled, and every mountain and hill brought low; and the crooked shall be made straight, and the rough into smooth ways; and all flesh shall see the salvation of God."[5] There is therefore one and the same God, the Father of our Lord, who also promised, through the prophets, that He would send His forerunner; and His salvation—that is, His Word—He caused to be made visible to all flesh, [the Word] Himself being made incarnate, that in all things their King might become manifest. For it is necessary that those [beings] which are judged do see the judge, and know Him from whom they receive judgment; and it is also proper, that those which follow on to

> glory should know Him who bestows upon them the gift of glory.[76]"

Again, the affirmation of one God while also affirming the distinctive persons of Father and Son as both God.

- "And then, [speaking of His] baptism, Matthew says, "The heavens were opened, and He saw the Spirit of God, as a dove, coming upon Him: and lo a voice from heaven, saying, This is my beloved Son, in whom I am well pleased." For Christ did not at that time descend upon Jesus, neither was Christ one and Jesus another: but the Word of God—who is the Saviour of all, and the ruler of heaven and earth, who is Jesus, as I have already pointed out, who did also take upon Him flesh, and was anointed by the Spirit from the Father—was made Jesus Christ, as Esaias also says, "There shall come forth a rod from the root of Jesse, and a flower shall rise from his root; and the Spirit of God shall rest upon Him: the spirit of

---

[76] Irenaeus of Lyons, "Irenæus against Heresies," in *The Apostolic Fathers with Justin Martyr and Irenaeus*, ed. Alexander Roberts, James Donaldson, and A. Cleveland Coxe, vol. 1, The Ante-Nicene Fathers (Buffalo, NY: Christian Literature Company, 1885), 422.

wisdom and understanding, the spirit of counsel and might, the spirit of knowledge and piety, and the spirit of the fear of God, shall fill Him. He shall not judge according to glory, nor reprove after the manner of speech; but He shall dispense judgment to the humble man, and reprove the haughty ones of the earth."[8] And again Esaias, pointing out beforehand His unction, and the reason why he was anointed, does himself say, "The Spirit of God is upon Me, because He hath anointed Me: He hath sent Me to preach the Gospel to the lowly, to heal the broken up in heart, to proclaim liberty to the captives, and sight to the blind; to announce the acceptable year of the Lord, and the day of vengeance; to comfort all that mourn." For inasmuch as the Word of God was man from the root of Jesse, and son of Abraham, in this respect did the Spirit of God rest upon Him, and anoint Him to preach the Gospel to the lowly. But inasmuch as He was God, He did not judge according to glory, nor reprove after the manner of speech. For "He needed not that any should testify to Him of man, for He Himself knew what was in man."[11] For He called all men that mourn; and granting forgiveness to those who had been led into captivity by their sins, He loosed them from their chains, of whom

> Solomon says, "Every one shall be holden with the cords of his own sins." Therefore did the Spirit of God descend upon Him, [the Spirit] of Him who had promised by the prophets that He would anoint Him, so that we, receiving from the abundance of His unction, might be saved. Such, then, [is the witness] of Matthew.[77]"

While never using the term "Trinity" this shows the Trinitarian faith of Irenaeus, one who was acquainted with some of the apostles and was a disciple of Polycarp, who was a disciple of the apostle John.

- "For "no man," he says, "hath seen God at any time," unless "the only-begotten Son of God, which is in the bosom of the Father, He hath declared [Him]." For He, the Son who is in His bosom, declares to all the Father who is invisible. Wherefore *they* know Him to whom the Son reveals Him; and again, the Father, by means of the Son, gives knowledge of His Son to those who love Him. By whom also Nathanael, being taught, recognised [Him], he to whom also the Lord bare

---

[77] Irenaeus of Lyons, "Irenæus against Heresies," in *The Apostolic Fathers with Justin Martyr and Irenaeus*, ed. Alexander Roberts, James Donaldson, and A. Cleveland Coxe, vol. 1, The Ante-Nicene Fathers (Buffalo, NY: Christian Literature Company, 1885), 423.

> witness, that he was "an Israelite indeed, in whom was no guile." The Israelite recognised his King, therefore did he cry out to Him, "Rabbi, Thou art the Son of God, Thou art the King of Israel." By whom also Peter, having been taught, recognised Christ as the Son of the living God, when [God] said, "Behold My dearly beloved Son, in whom I am well pleased: I will put my Spirit upon Him, and He shall show judgment to the Gentiles. He shall not strive, nor cry; neither shall any man hear His voice in the streets. A bruised reed shall He not break, and smoking flax shall He not quench, until He send forth judgment into contention; and in His name shall the Gentiles trust."[278]

Once again, we see the distinction between the Divine Persons affirmed by one who held to the one true God.

- Such, then, are the first principles of the Gospel: that there is one God, the Maker of this universe; He who was also announced by the prophets, and who by

[78] Irenaeus of Lyons, "Irenæus against Heresies," in *The Apostolic Fathers with Justin Martyr and Irenaeus*, ed. Alexander Roberts, James Donaldson, and A. Cleveland Coxe, vol. 1, The Ante-Nicene Fathers (Buffalo, NY: Christian Literature Company, 1885), 427–428.

> Moses set forth the dispensation of the law,—[principles] which proclaim the Father of our Lord Jesus Christ, and ignore any other God or Father except Him.[79]"

Irenaeus has established his belief in one God as well as teaching the distinction between the Divine Persons. Here he states it is a fundamental of gospel faith that there is one God. That is the essence of Trinitarian doctrine, that there is one God who is three persons.

- "The Apostle Peter, therefore, after the resurrection of the Lord, and His assumption into the heavens, being desirous of filling up the number of the twelve apostles, and in electing into the place of Judas any substitute who should be chosen by God, thus addressed those who were present: "Men [and] brethren, this Scripture must needs have been fulfilled, which the Holy Ghost, by the mouth of David, spake before concerning Judas, which was made guide to them that took Jesus. For he was numbered with us: … Let his habitation be desolate, and let no man dwell

---

[79] Irenaeus of Lyons, "Irenæus against Heresies," in *The Apostolic Fathers with Justin Martyr and Irenaeus*, ed. Alexander Roberts, James Donaldson, and A. Cleveland Coxe, vol. 1, The Ante-Nicene Fathers (Buffalo, NY: Christian Literature Company, 1885), 428.

> therein; and, His bishoprick let another take;"[2]—thus leading to the completion of the apostles, according to the words spoken by David. Again, when the Holy Ghost had descended upon the disciples, that they all might prophesy and speak with tongues, and some mocked them, as if drunken with new wine, Peter said that they were not drunken, for it was the third hour of the day; but that this was what had been spoken by the prophet: "It shall come to pass in the last days, saith God, I will pour out of my Spirit upon all flesh, and they shall prophesy." The God, therefore, who did promise by the prophet, that He would send His Spirit upon the whole human race, was He who did send; and God Himself is announced by Peter as having fulfilled His own promise.[80]"

Here we can see the person and deity of the Holy Ghost proclaimed in Trinitarian theology, as the Holy Ghost spoke and His Word is declared to be God's promise.

---

[80] Irenaeus of Lyons, "Irenæus against Heresies," in *The Apostolic Fathers with Justin Martyr and Irenaeus*, ed. Alexander Roberts, James Donaldson, and A. Cleveland Coxe, vol. 1, The Ante-Nicene Fathers (Buffalo, NY: Christian Literature Company, 1885), 429–430.

- Peter says to them, "Repent, and be baptized every one of you in the name of Jesus for the remission of sins, and ye shall receive the gift of the Holy Ghost." Thus the apostles did not preach another God, or another Fulness; nor, that the Christ who suffered and rose again was one, while he who flew off on high was another, and remained impossible; but that there was one and the same God the Father, and Christ Jesus who rose from the dead; and they preached faith in Him, to those who did not believe on the Son of God, and exhorted them out of the prophets, that the Christ whom God promised to send, He sent in Jesus, whom they crucified and God raised up.[81]"

Again, the apostolic preaching is shown to present the personal distinction between the Father and the Son while affirming one God.

- "The whole Church, it is then said, "when they had heard that, lifted up the voice to God with one accord, and said, Lord, Thou art God, which hast made heaven,

---

[81] Irenaeus of Lyons, "Irenæus against Heresies," in *The Apostolic Fathers with Justin Martyr and Irenaeus*, ed. Alexander Roberts, James Donaldson, and A. Cleveland Coxe, vol. 1, The Ante-Nicene Fathers (Buffalo, NY: Christian Literature Company, 1885), 430.

and earth, and the sea, and all that in them is; who, through the Holy Ghost, by the mouth of our father David, Thy servant, hast said, Why did the heathen rage, and the people imagine vain things? The kings of the earth stood up, and the rulers were gathered together against the Lord, and against His Christ. For of a truth, in this city, against Thy holy Son Jesus, whom Thou hast anointed, both Herod and Pontius Pilate, with the Gentiles, and the people of Israel, were gathered together, to do whatsoever Thy hand and Thy counsel determined before to be done." These [are the] voices of the Church from which every Church had its origin; these are the voices of the metropolis of the citizens of the new covenant; these are the voices of the apostles; these are voices of the disciples of the Lord, the truly perfect, who, after the assumption of the Lord, were perfected by the Spirit, and called upon the God who made heaven, and earth, and the sea,—who was announced by the prophets,—and Jesus Christ His Son, whom God anointed, and who knew no other [God].[82]"

---

[82] Irenaeus of Lyons, "Irenæus against Heresies," in *The Apostolic Fathers with Justin Martyr and Irenaeus*, ed. Alexander Roberts, James Donaldson, and A. Cleveland

Irenaeus' declaration of the apostolic doctrine of the early churches was one which affirmed the essential Deity of Christ as God and His unity with yet distinction from the Father. In other words, he affirmed the early churches believed in one God while also holding to faith in the personal distinctions in the One God.

- "But that both the apostles and their disciples thus taught as the Church preaches, and thus teaching were perfected, wherefore also they were called away to that which is perfect—Stephen, teaching these truths, when he was yet on earth, saw the glory of God, and Jesus on His right hand, and exclaimed, "Behold, I see the heavens opened, and the Son of man standing on the right hand of God." These words he said, and was stoned; and thus did he fulfil the perfect doctrine, copying in every respect the Leader of martyrdom, and praying for those who were slaying him, in these words: "Lord, lay not this sin to their charge." Thus were they perfected who knew one and the same God, who from beginning to end was present with mankind in the various dispensations; as the prophet Hosea declares: "I have filled up visions, and used similitudes by the hands of the prophets."[4] Those,

---

Coxe, vol. 1, The Ante-Nicene Fathers (Buffalo, NY: Christian Literature Company, 1885), 431.

> therefore, who delivered up their souls to death for Christ's Gospel—how could they have spoken to men in accordance with old-established opinion? If this had been the course adopted by them, they should not have suffered; but inasmuch as they did preach things contrary to those persons who did not assent to the truth, for that reason they suffered. It is evident, therefore, that they did not relinquish the truth, but with all boldness preached to the Jews and Greeks. To the Jews, indeed, [they proclaimed] that the Jesus who was crucified by them was the Son of God, the Judge of quick and dead, and that He has received from His Father an eternal kingdom in Israel, as I have pointed out; but to the Greeks they preached one God, who made all things, and Jesus Christ His Son.[83]"

Irenaeus understood the Son literally stood on the right hand of God. Here again we see Trinitarian theology on full display, as the Divine Persons of the One True God are distinguished.

---

[83] Irenaeus of Lyons, "Irenæus against Heresies," in *The Apostolic Fathers with Justin Martyr and Irenaeus*, ed. Alexander Roberts, James Donaldson, and A. Cleveland Coxe, vol. 1, The Ante-Nicene Fathers (Buffalo, NY: Christian Literature Company, 1885), 435.

- “But it is evident from Peter’s words that he did indeed still retain the God who was already known to them; but he also bare witness to them that Jesus Christ was the Son of God, the Judge of quick and dead, into whom he did also command them to be baptized for the remission of sins; and not this alone, but he witnessed that Jesus was Himself the Son of God, who also, having been anointed with the Holy Spirit, is called Jesus Christ. And He is the same being that was born of Mary, as the testimony of Peter implies. Can it really be, that Peter was not at that time as yet in possession of the perfect knowledge which these men discovered afterwards? According to them, therefore, Peter was imperfect, and the rest of the apostles were imperfect; and so it would be fitting that they, coming to life again, should become disciples of these men, in order that they too might be made perfect. But this is truly ridiculous. These men, in fact, are proved to be not disciples of the apostles, but of their own wicked notions. To this cause also are due the various opinions which exist among them, inasmuch as each one adopted error just as he was capable [of embracing it]. But the Church throughout all the world, having its origin firm from the apostles,

perseveres in one and the same opinion with regard to God and His Son.
But again: Whom did Philip preach to the eunuch of the queen of the Ethiopians, returning from Jerusalem, and reading Esaias the prophet, when he and this man were alone together? Was it not He of whom the prophet spoke: "He was led as a sheep to the slaughter, and as a lamb dumb before the shearer, so He opened not the mouth?" "But who shall declare His nativity? for His life shall be taken away from the earth." [Philip declared] that this was Jesus, and that the Scripture was fulfilled in Him; as did also the believing eunuch himself: and, immediately requesting to be baptized, he said, "I believe Jesus Christ to be the Son of God." This man was also sent into the regions of Ethiopia, to preach what he had himself believed, that there was one God preached by the prophets, but that the Son of this [God] had already made [His] appearance in human nature (*secundum hominem*), and had been led as a sheep to the slaughter; and all the other statements which the prophets made regarding Him.[84]"

---

[84] Irenaeus of Lyons, "Irenæus against Heresies," in *The Apostolic Fathers with Justin Martyr and Irenaeus*, ed.

Irenaeus' declaration here is that there is One True God and Jesus Christ is His Son, being of the same essence as the Father yet distinct from Him in person.

- "There is therefore, as I have pointed out, one God the Father, and one Christ Jesus, who came by means of the whole dispensational arrangements [connected with Him], and gathered together all things in Himself. But in every respect, too, He is man, the formation of God; and thus He took up man into Himself, the invisible becoming visible, the incomprehensible being made comprehensible, the impassible becoming capable of suffering, and the Word being made man, thus summing up all things in Himself: so that as in super-celestial, spiritual, and invisible things, the Word of God is supreme, so also in things visible and corporeal He might possess the supremacy, and, taking to Himself the pre-eminence, as well as constituting Himself Head of the Church, He might draw all things to Himself at the proper time.

Alexander Roberts, James Donaldson, and A. Cleveland Coxe, vol. 1, The Ante-Nicene Fathers (Buffalo, NY: Christian Literature Company, 1885), 433.

> With Him is nothing incomplete or out of due season, just as with the Father there is nothing incongruous. For all these things were foreknown by the Father; but the Son works them out at the proper time in perfect order and sequence.[85]"

Once again, this second century Christian preacher, disciple of the apostles, declares both the Deity of Christ as equal to the Father as well as His personal distinction from the Father.

- "And again, the angel said, when bringing good tidings to Mary: "He shall be great, and shall be called the Son of the Highest; and the Lord shall give unto Him the throne of His father David;" acknowledging that He who is the Son of the Highest, the same is Himself also the Son of David. And David, knowing by the Spirit the dispensation of the advent of this Person, by which He is supreme over all the living and dead, confessed Him as

---

85 Irenaeus of Lyons, "Irenæus against Heresies," in *The Apostolic Fathers with Justin Martyr and Irenaeus*, ed. Alexander Roberts, James Donaldson, and A. Cleveland Coxe, vol. 1, The Ante-Nicene Fathers (Buffalo, NY: Christian Literature Company, 1885), 442–443.

> Lord, sitting on the right hand of the Most High Father.[86]"

There is again to be seen the distinction maintained between the persons of the Father and the Son as the Son is seated at the right hand of the Father.

- "they thus wander from the truth, because their doctrine departs from Him who is truly God, being ignorant that His only-begotten Word, who is always present with the human race, united to and mingled with His own creation, according to the Father's pleasure, and who became flesh, is Himself Jesus Christ our Lord, who did also suffer for us, and rose again on our behalf, and who will come again in the glory of His Father, to raise up all flesh, and for the manifestation of salvation, and to apply the rule of just judgment to all who were made by Him. There is therefore, as I have pointed out, one God the Father, and one Christ Jesus, who came by means of the whole dispensational arrangements [connected

---

[86] Irenaeus of Lyons, "Irenæus against Heresies," in *The Apostolic Fathers with Justin Martyr and Irenaeus*, ed. Alexander Roberts, James Donaldson, and A. Cleveland Coxe, vol. 1, The Ante-Nicene Fathers (Buffalo, NY: Christian Literature Company, 1885), 441.

with Him], and gathered together all things in Himself.[87]"

Again, long before there was a Roman Catholic Church, there was the affirmation of the one God with Jesus being a distinct Divine Person Who is God but is not the Father.

- "For all these things were foreknown by the Father; but the Son works them out at the proper time in perfect order and sequence. [88]" "Paul also says: "But when the fulness of time came, God sent forth His Son." By which is made manifest, that all things which had been foreknown of the Father, our Lord did accomplish in their order, season, and hour, foreknown and fitting, being indeed one and the

[87] Irenaeus of Lyons, "Irenæus against Heresies," in *The Apostolic Fathers with Justin Martyr and Irenaeus*, ed. Alexander Roberts, James Donaldson, and A. Cleveland Coxe, vol. 1, The Ante-Nicene Fathers (Buffalo, NY: Christian Literature Company, 1885), 442–443.

[88] Irenaeus of Lyons, "Irenæus against Heresies," in *The Apostolic Fathers with Justin Martyr and Irenaeus*, ed. Alexander Roberts, James Donaldson, and A. Cleveland Coxe, vol. 1, The Ante-Nicene Fathers (Buffalo, NY: Christian Literature Company, 1885), 443.

same, but rich and great. For He fulfils the bountiful and comprehensive will of His Father, inasmuch as He is Himself the Saviour of those who are saved, and the Lord of those who are under authority, and the God of all those things which have been formed, the only-begotten of the Father, Christ who was announced, and the Word of God, who became incarnate when the fulness of time had come, at which the Son of God had to become the Son of man.[89]"

Note the Divine arrangement in which the Father ordains and the Son works, thus showing a distinction between the persons.

- Jesus Christ, the Son of God, is one and the same, who did by suffering reconcile us to God, and rose from the dead; who is at the right hand of the Father, and perfect in all things; "who, when He was buffeted, struck not in return; who, when He suffered, threatened not;" and when He underwent tyranny, He prayed His

---

[89] Irenaeus of Lyons, "Irenæus against Heresies," in *The Apostolic Fathers with Justin Martyr and Irenaeus*, ed. Alexander Roberts, James Donaldson, and A. Cleveland Coxe, vol. 1, The Ante-Nicene Fathers (Buffalo, NY: Christian Literature Company, 1885), 443.

> Father that He would forgive those who had crucified Him. For He did Himself truly bring in salvation: since He is Himself the Word of God, Himself the Only-begotten of the Father, Christ Jesus our Lord.[90]"

Once again, Irenaeus affirms the personal distinction between the Father and the Son, while affirming the essential Deity of Christ and thus the unity of the Godhead.

- "1. It certainly was in the power of the apostles to declare that Christ descended upon Jesus, or that the so-called superior Saviour [came down] upon the dispensational one, or he who is from the invisible places upon him from the Demiurge; but they neither knew nor said anything of the kind: for, had they known it, they would have also certainly stated it. But what really was the case, that did they record, [namely,] that the Spirit of God as a dove descended upon Him; this Spirit, of whom it was declared by Isaiah, "And

---

[90] Irenaeus of Lyons, "Irenæus against Heresies," in *The Apostolic Fathers with Justin Martyr and Irenaeus*, ed. Alexander Roberts, James Donaldson, and A. Cleveland Coxe, vol. 1, The Ante-Nicene Fathers (Buffalo, NY: Christian Literature Company, 1885), 444.

the Spirit of God shall rest upon Him," as I have already said. And again: "The Spirit of the Lord is upon Me, because He hath anointed Me." That is the Spirit of whom the Lord declares, "For it is not ye that speak, but the Spirit of your Father which speaketh in you." And again, giving to the disciples the power of regeneration into God,[10] He said to them, "Go and teach all nations, baptizing them in the name of the Father, and of the Son, and of the Holy Ghost." For [God] promised, that in the last times He would pour Him [the Spirit] upon [His] servants and handmaids, that they might prophesy; wherefore He did also descend upon the Son of God, made the Son of man, becoming accustomed in fellowship with Him to dwell in the human race, to rest with human beings, and to dwell in the workmanship of God, working the will of the Father in them, and renewing them from their old habits into the newness of Christ.

2. This Spirit did David ask for the human race, saying, "And stablish me with Thine all-governing Spirit;" who also, as Luke says, descended at the day of Pentecost upon the disciples after the Lord's ascension, having power to admit all nations to the entrance of life, and to the opening of the new covenant; from

whence also, with one accord in all languages, they uttered praise to God, the Spirit bringing distant tribes to unity, and offering to the Father the first-fruits of all nations. Wherefore also the Lord promised to send the Comforter, who should join us to God. "[91]

The distinction of the Divine Persons is even more explicitly shown here when the writer speaks of the Spirit personally, saying, "who," of Him. Nowhere in this does Irenaeus speak of a god who is one person or of three gods: He speaks of three Persons in One Being Who is God. Again, this was written three centuries before the first pope, Leo, and thus centuries before the Roman Catholic Church came into existence.

- "The Lord, receiving this as a gift from His Father, does Himself also confer it upon those who are partakers of Himself, sending the Holy Spirit upon all the earth.[92]"

---

[91] Irenaeus of Lyons, "Irenæus against Heresies," in *The Apostolic Fathers with Justin Martyr and Irenaeus*, ed. Alexander Roberts, James Donaldson, and A. Cleveland Coxe, vol. 1, The Ante-Nicene Fathers (Buffalo, NY: Christian Literature Company, 1885), 444.

[92] Irenaeus of Lyons, "Irenæus against Heresies," in *The Apostolic Fathers with Justin Martyr and Irenaeus*, ed.

Here we again see the Lord, the Father, and the Holy Spirit as distinct.

- As it has been clearly demonstrated that the Word, who existed in the beginning with God, by whom all things were made, who was also always present with mankind, was in these last days, according to the time appointed by the Father, united to His own workmanship, inasmuch as He became a man liable to suffering, [it follows] that every objection is set aside of those who say, "If our Lord was born at that time, Christ had therefore no previous existence." For I have shown that the Son of God did not then begin to exist, being with the Father from the beginning; but when He became incarnate, and was made man, He commenced afresh the long line of human beings, and furnished us, in a brief, comprehensive manner, with salvation; so that what we had lost in Adam—namely, to be according to the image and likeness

---

Alexander Roberts, James Donaldson, and A. Cleveland Coxe, vol. 1, The Ante-Nicene Fathers (Buffalo, NY: Christian Literature Company, 1885), 445.

of God—that we might recover in Christ Jesus.[93]

Irenaeus taught the essential Deity of Jesus the Son of God, the Word, as He existed in eternity before the Creation and was distinct from the Father eternally, being present with Him eternally.

- "For the one and the same Spirit of God, who proclaimed by the prophets what and of what sort the advent of the Lord should be, did by these elders give a just interpretation of what had been truly prophesied; and He did Himself, by the apostles, announce that the fulness of the times of the adoption had arrived, that the kingdom of heaven had drawn nigh, and that *He* was dwelling within those that believe on Him who was born Emmanuel of the Virgin. [94]"

---

[93] Irenaeus of Lyons, "Irenæus against Heresies," in *The Apostolic Fathers with Justin Martyr and Irenaeus*, ed. Alexander Roberts, James Donaldson, and A. Cleveland Coxe, vol. 1, The Ante-Nicene Fathers (Buffalo, NY: Christian Literature Company, 1885), 445–446.

[94] Irenaeus of Lyons, "Irenæus against Heresies," in *The Apostolic Fathers with Justin Martyr and Irenaeus*, ed. Alexander Roberts, James Donaldson, and A. Cleveland

The distinct Divine person of the Holy Ghost is presented here as it was He by whom the Word came to and through the prophets *2 Peter 1:19-21*.

- "Carefully, then, has the Holy Ghost pointed out, by what has been said, His birth from a virgin, and His essence, that He is God (for the name Emmanuel indicates this). And He shows that He is a man, when He says, "Butter and honey shall He eat;" and in that He terms Him a child also, [in saying,] "before He knows good and evil;" for these are all the tokens of a human infant. But that He "will not consent to evil, that He may choose that which is good,"—this is proper to God; that by the fact, that He shall eat butter and honey, we should not understand that He is a mere man only, nor, on the other hand, from the name Emmanuel, should suspect Him to be God without flesh.[95]"

Coxe, vol. 1, The Ante-Nicene Fathers (Buffalo, NY: Christian Literature Company, 1885), 452.

[95] Irenaeus of Lyons, "Irenæus against Heresies," in *The Apostolic Fathers with Justin Martyr and Irenaeus*, ed. Alexander Roberts, James Donaldson, and A. Cleveland Coxe, vol. 1, The Ante-Nicene Fathers (Buffalo, NY: Christian Literature Company, 1885), 452.

Here we see the plain distinction between the Son and the Spirit presented to us, with both being spoken of as persons.

- "Now man is a mixed organization of soul and flesh, who was formed after the likeness of God, and moulded by His hands, that is, by the Son and Holy Spirit, to whom also He said, "Let Us make man."[96]"

God, Son, Spirit distinct yet One and all three as the One True God created man.

- "Again, our Lord Jesus Christ confesses this same Being as His Father, where He says: "I confess to thee, O Father, Lord of heaven and earth." What Father will those men have us to understand [by these words], those who are most perverse sophists of Pandora? Whether shall it be Bythus, whom they have fabled of

---

[96] Irenaeus of Lyons, "Irenæus against Heresies," in *The Apostolic Fathers with Justin Martyr and Irenaeus*, ed. Alexander Roberts, James Donaldson, and A. Cleveland Coxe, vol. 1, The Ante-Nicene Fathers (Buffalo, NY: Christian Literature Company, 1885), 463.

themselves; or their Mother; or the Only-begotten? Or shall it be he whom the Marcionites or the others have invented as god (whom I indeed have amply demonstrated to be no god at all); or shall it be (what is really the case) the Maker of heaven and earth, whom also the prophets proclaimed,—whom Christ, too, confesses as His Father,—whom also the law announces, saying: "Hear, O Israel; The Lord thy God is one God?"[97]"

Irenaeus has already established his faith in one true God and Christ as being God. Now he speaks of Christ and the Father as distinct, with the Son confessing His Father, thus showing his belief in the distinction of persons in God.

- "Well spake he, who said that the unmeasurable Father was Himself subjected to measure in the Son; for

[97] Irenaeus of Lyons, "Irenæus against Heresies," in *The Apostolic Fathers with Justin Martyr and Irenaeus*, ed. Alexander Roberts, James Donaldson, and A. Cleveland Coxe, vol. 1, The Ante-Nicene Fathers (Buffalo, NY: Christian Literature Company, 1885), 463–464.

the Son is the measure of the Father, since He also comprehends Him.[98]"

In brief, he is saying the Son is Divine and equal to the Father, yet distinct.

- "Christ Himself, therefore, together with the Father, is the God of the living, who spake to Moses, and who was also manifested to the fathers.[99]"

Notice how Irenaeus affirms the deity of Christ, His union with the Father as God, and His distinction from the Father in His Divine person.

- "For the Lord, revealing Himself to His disciples, that He Himself is the Word, who imparts knowledge of the

---

[98] Irenaeus of Lyons, "Irenæus against Heresies," in *The Apostolic Fathers with Justin Martyr and Irenaeus*, ed. Alexander Roberts, James Donaldson, and A. Cleveland Coxe, vol. 1, The Ante-Nicene Fathers (Buffalo, NY: Christian Literature Company, 1885), 466.

[99] Irenaeus of Lyons, "Irenæus against Heresies," in *The Apostolic Fathers with Justin Martyr and Irenaeus*, ed. Alexander Roberts, James Donaldson, and A. Cleveland Coxe, vol. 1, The Ante-Nicene Fathers (Buffalo, NY: Christian Literature Company, 1885), 467.

Father, and reproving the Jews, who imagined that they, had [the knowledge of] God, while they nevertheless rejected His Word, through whom God is made known, declared, "No man knoweth the Son, but the Father; neither knoweth any man the Father, save the Son, and he to whom the Son has willed to reveal [Him]." Thus hath Matthew set it down, and Luke in like manner, and Mark the very same; for John omits this passage. They, however, who would be wiser than the apostles, write [the verse] in the following manner: "No man *knew* the Father, but the Son; nor the Son, but the Father, and he to whom the Son has willed to reveal [Him];" and they explain it as if the true God were known to none prior to our Lord's advent; and that God who was announced by the prophets, they allege not to be the Father of Christ.[100]"

---

[100] Irenaeus of Lyons, "Irenæus against Heresies," in *The Apostolic Fathers with Justin Martyr and Irenaeus*, ed. Alexander Roberts, James Donaldson, and A. Cleveland Coxe, vol. 1, The Ante-Nicene Fathers (Buffalo, NY: Christian Literature Company, 1885), 467–468.

Irenaeus once again Biblically presents to us the personal distinction between the Father and the Son.

- "For no one can know the Father, unless through the Word of God, that is, unless by the Son revealing [Him]; neither can he have knowledge of the Son, unless through the good pleasure of the Father. But the Son performs the good pleasure of the Father; for the Father sends, and the Son is sent, and comes. And His Word knows that His Father is, as far as regards us, invisible and infinite; and since He cannot be declared [by any one else], He does Himself declare Him to us; and, on the other hand, it is the Father alone who knows His own Word. And both these truths has our Lord declared. Wherefore the Son reveals the knowledge of the Father through His own manifestation. For the manifestation of the Son is the knowledge of the Father; for all things are manifested through the Word. In order, therefore, that we might know that the Son who came is He who imparts to those believing on Him a knowledge of the Father, He said to His disciples: "No man knoweth the Son but the Father, nor the Father but

> the Son, and those to whomsoever the Son shall reveal Him;" thus setting Himself forth and the Father as He [really] is, that we may not receive any other Father, except Him who is revealed by the Son.[101]"

Having already affirmed his faith in One God; Irenaeus again demonstrates his belief in the personal distinction between God the Father and God the Son.

- "For by means of the creation itself, the Word reveals God the Creator; and by means of the world [does He declare] the Lord the Maker of the world; and by means of the formation [of man] the Artificer who formed him; and by the Son that Father who begat the Son: and these things do indeed address all men in the same manner, but all do not in the same way believe them. But by the law and the prophets did the Word preach both Himself and the Father alike [to all]; and all the people heard Him alike,

---

[101] Irenaeus of Lyons, "Irenæus against Heresies," in *The Apostolic Fathers with Justin Martyr and Irenaeus*, ed. Alexander Roberts, James Donaldson, and A. Cleveland Coxe, vol. 1, The Ante-Nicene Fathers (Buffalo, NY: Christian Literature Company, 1885), 468.

> but all did not alike believe. And through the Word Himself who had been made visible and palpable, was the Father shown forth, although all did not equally believe in Him; but all saw the Father in the Son: for the Father is the invisible of the Son, but the Son the visible of the Father. And for this reason all spake with Christ when He was present [upon earth], and they named Him God. Yea, even the demons exclaimed, on beholding the Son: "We know Thee who Thou art, the Holy One of God." And the devil looking at Him, and tempting Him, said: "If Thou art the Son of God;"—all thus indeed seeing and speaking of the Son and the Father, but all not believing [in them].[102]"

Jesus named God and Creator yet spoken of as being distinct from the Father in His person.

- "He, therefore, who was known, was not a different being from Him who

[102] Irenaeus of Lyons, "Irenæus against Heresies," in *The Apostolic Fathers with Justin Martyr and Irenaeus*, ed. Alexander Roberts, James Donaldson, and A. Cleveland Coxe, vol. 1, The Ante-Nicene Fathers (Buffalo, NY: Christian Literature Company, 1885), 469.

declared, "No man knoweth the Father," but one and the same, the Father making all things subject to Him; while He received testimony from all that He was very man, and that He was very God, from the Father, from the Spirit, from angels, from the creation itself, from men, from apostate spirits and demons, from the enemy, and last of all, from death itself. But the Son, administering all things for the Father, works from the beginning even to the end, and without Him no man can attain the knowledge of God. For the Son is the knowledge of the Father; but the knowledge of the Son is in the Father, and has been revealed through the Son; and this was the reason why the Lord declared: "No man knoweth the Son, but the Father; nor the Father, save the Son, and those to whomsoever the Son shall reveal [Him]." For "shall reveal" was said not with reference to the future alone, as if then [only] the Word had begun to manifest the Father when He was born of Mary, but it applies indifferently throughout all time. For the Son, being present with His own handiwork from the beginning, reveals the Father to all; to whom He wills, and when He wills, and as the Father wills. Wherefore, then, in all things, and through all things, there is one God, the Father, and one Word, and one Son, and one Spirit, and one salvation to all who believe in Him.[103]"

The essential nature and substance of the Father and Son are the same. Yet they are spoken of distinctly as persons. Furthermore, God- "Him"- is expressly spoken of as God, the Father, Son/Word, and Spirit, being distinctly three in one "Him."

- "In the beginning, therefore, did God form Adam, not as if He stood in need of man, but that He might have [some one] upon whom to confer His benefits. For not alone antecedently to Adam, but also before all creation, the Word glorified His Father, remaining in Him; and was Himself glorified by the Father, as He did Himself declare, "Father, glorify Thou Me with the

---

[103] Irenaeus of Lyons, "Irenæus against Heresies," in *The Apostolic Fathers with Justin Martyr and Irenaeus*, ed. Alexander Roberts, James Donaldson, and A. Cleveland Coxe, vol. 1, The Ante-Nicene Fathers (Buffalo, NY: Christian Literature Company, 1885), 469.

glory which I had with Thee before the world was."[104]"

Irenaeus here presents the eternal distinction between the Father and Son as well as their union and unity of being, as shown in Scripture, being before Creation and time.

- "But what other name is there which is glorified among the Gentiles than that of our Lord, by whom the Father is glorified, and man also? And because it is [the name] of His own Son, who was made man by Him, He calls it His own. Just as a king, if he himself paints a likeness of his son, is right in calling this likeness his own, for both these reasons, because it is [the likeness] of his son, and because it is his own production; so also does the Father confess the name of Jesus Christ, which is throughout all the world glorified in the Church, to be His own, both because it is that of His Son, and because He who thus

---

[104] Irenaeus of Lyons, "Irenæus against Heresies," in *The Apostolic Fathers with Justin Martyr and Irenaeus*, ed. Alexander Roberts, James Donaldson, and A. Cleveland Coxe, vol. 1, The Ante-Nicene Fathers (Buffalo, NY: Christian Literature Company, 1885), 478.

> describes it gave Him for the salvation of men. Since, therefore, the name of the Son belongs to the Father, and since in the omnipotent God the Church makes offerings through Jesus Christ, He says well on both these grounds, "And in every place incense is offered to My name, and a pure sacrifice." Now John, in the Apocalypse, declares that the "incense" is "the prayers of the saints."[105]"

The one name is due to the unity of nature, yet there remains the distinction of persons. Thus Irenaeus.

- "For with Him were always present the Word and Wisdom, the Son and the Spirit, by whom and in whom, freely and spontaneously, He made all things, to whom also He speaks, saying, "Let Us make man after Our image and likeness;" He taking from Himself the substance of the creatures [formed], and the pattern of things

---

[105] Irenaeus of Lyons, "Irenæus against Heresies," in *The Apostolic Fathers with Justin Martyr and Irenaeus*, ed. Alexander Roberts, James Donaldson, and A. Cleveland Coxe, vol. 1, The Ante-Nicene Fathers (Buffalo, NY: Christian Literature Company, 1885), 484.

made, and the type of all the adornments in the world.[106]"

- "Truly, then, the Scripture declared, which says, "First of all believe that there is one God, who has established all things, and completed them, and having caused that from what had no being, all things should come into existence:" He who contains all things, and is Himself contained by no one. Rightly also has Malachi said among the prophets: "Is it not one God who hath established us? Have we not all one Father?" In accordance with this, too, does the apostle say, "There is one God, the Father, who is above all, and in us all." Likewise does the Lord also say: "All things are delivered to Me by My Father;" manifestly by Him who made all things; for He did not deliver to Him the things of another, but His own. But in *all things* [it is implied that]

---

106 Irenaeus of Lyons, "Irenæus against Heresies," in *The Apostolic Fathers with Justin Martyr and Irenaeus*, ed. Alexander Roberts, James Donaldson, and A. Cleveland Coxe, vol. 1, The Ante-Nicene Fathers (Buffalo, NY: Christian Literature Company, 1885), 487–488.

nothing has been kept back [from Him], and for this reason the same person is the Judge of the living and the dead; "having the key of David: He shall open, and no man shall shut: He shall shut, and no man shall open." For no one was able, either in heaven or in earth, or under the earth, to open the book of the Father, or to behold Him, with the exception of the Lamb who was slain, and who redeemed us with His own blood, receiving power over all things from the same God who made all things by the Word, and adorned them by [His] Wisdom, when "the Word was made flesh;" that even as the Word of God had the sovereignty in the heavens, so also might He have the sovereignty in earth, inasmuch as [He was] a righteous man, "who did no sin, neither was there found guile in His mouth;" and that He might have the pre-eminence over those things which are under the earth, He Himself being made "the first-begotten of the dead;"[8] and that all things, as I have already said, might behold their King; and that the paternal light might meet with and rest upon the flesh of our Lord, and come to us from His resplendent flesh, and that thus man might attain to immortality, having been invested with the paternal light.

I have also largely demonstrated, that the Word, namely the Son, was always with the Father; and that Wisdom also, which is the Spirit, was present with Him, anterior to all creation, He declares by Solomon: "God by Wisdom founded the earth, and by understanding hath He established the heaven. By His knowledge the depths burst forth, and the clouds dropped down the dew." And again: "The Lord created me the beginning of His ways in His work: He set me up from everlasting, in the beginning, before He made the earth, before He established the depths, and before the fountains of waters gushed forth; before the mountains were made strong, and before all the hills, He brought me forth."[10] And again: "When He prepared the heaven, I was with Him, and when He established the fountains of the deep; when He made the foundations of the earth strong, I was with Him preparing [them]. I was He in whom He rejoiced, and throughout all time I was daily glad before His face, when He rejoiced at the completion of the world, and was delighted in the sons of men."[107]

There cannot be a much plainer Trinitarian statement than this.

- "Wherefore the prophets, receiving the prophetic gift from the same Word, announced His advent according to the flesh, by which the blending and communion of God and man took place according to the good pleasure of the Father, the Word of God foretelling from the beginning that God should be seen by men, and hold converse with them upon earth, should confer with them, and should be present with His own creation, saving it, and becoming capable of being perceived by it, and freeing us from the hands of all that hate us, that is, from every spirit of wickedness; and causing us to serve Him in holiness and righteousness all our

---

[107] Irenaeus of Lyons, "Irenæus against Heresies," in *The Apostolic Fathers with Justin Martyr and Irenaeus*, ed. Alexander Roberts, James Donaldson, and A. Cleveland Coxe, vol. 1, The Ante-Nicene Fathers (Buffalo, NY: Christian Literature Company, 1885), 488.

days, in order that man, having embraced the Spirit of God, might pass into the glory of the Father.[108]"

Here Irenaeus speaks of Jesus as Creator and God while personally distinguishing Him from the Father.

- "God is powerful in all things, having been seen at that time indeed, prophetically through the Spirit, and seen, too, adoptively through the Son; and He shall also be seen paternally in the kingdom of heaven, the Spirit truly preparing man in the Son of God, and the Son leading him to the Father, while the Father, too, confers [upon him] incorruption for eternal life, which comes to every one from the fact of his seeing God.[109]"

---

[108] Irenaeus of Lyons, "Irenæus against Heresies," in *The Apostolic Fathers with Justin Martyr and Irenaeus*, ed. Alexander Roberts, James Donaldson, and A. Cleveland Coxe, vol. 1, The Ante-Nicene Fathers (Buffalo, NY: Christian Literature Company, 1885), 488.

[109] Irenaeus of Lyons, "Irenæus against Heresies," in *The Apostolic Fathers with Justin Martyr and Irenaeus*, ed. Alexander Roberts, James Donaldson, and A. Cleveland

It is quite obvious Irenaeus believed in the personal distinctions between the Father, Son, and Spirit, and that is certainly on display in this passage. He speaks of God, the Spirit, and the Son, with the first being spoken of as the Father as he used the term, "paternal," regarding Him.

- "Thus, therefore, was God revealed; for God the Father is shown forth through all these [operations], the Spirit indeed working, and the Son ministering, while the Father was approving, and man's salvation being accomplished. As He also declares through Hosea the prophet: "I," He says, "have multiplied visions, and have used similitudes by the ministry (*in manibus*) of the prophets." But the apostle expounded this very passage, when he said, "Now there are diversities of gifts, but the same Spirit; and there are differences of ministrations, but the same Lord; and there are diversities of operations, but it is the same God which worketh all in all. But the manifestation of the Spirit is given to every man to profit

---

Coxe, vol. 1, The Ante-Nicene Fathers (Buffalo, NY: Christian Literature Company, 1885), 489.

withal." But as He who worketh all things in all is God, [as to the points] of what nature and how great He is, [God] is invisible and indescribable to all things which have been made by Him, but He is by no means unknown: for all things learn through His Word that there is one God the Father, who contains all things, and who grants existence to all, as is written in the Gospel: "No man hath seen God at any time, except the only-begotten Son, who is in the bosom of the Father; He has declared [Him.]"[110]"

Again, Irenaeus plainly speaks of the Father, Son, and Spirit as distinct persons doing distinct works.

- "By this arrangement, therefore, and these harmonies, and a sequence of this nature, man, a created and organized being, is rendered after the image and likeness of the uncreated God,—the Father planning everything well and giving His commands, the

---

[110] Irenaeus of Lyons, "Irenæus against Heresies," in *The Apostolic Fathers with Justin Martyr and Irenaeus*, ed. Alexander Roberts, James Donaldson, and A. Cleveland Coxe, vol. 1, The Ante-Nicene Fathers (Buffalo, NY: Christian Literature Company, 1885), 489.

Son carrying these into execution and performing the work of creating, and the Spirit nourishing and increasing [what is made], but man making progress day by day, and ascending towards the perfect, that is, approximating to the uncreated One.[111]"

This is a very plain presentation of Irenaeus' belief in the three distinct Persons of God as he describes their distinct yet perfectly united ministries.

- "FOR in no other way could we have learned the things of God, unless our Master, existing as the Word, had become man. For no other being had the power of revealing to us the things of the Father, except His own proper Word. For what other person "knew the mind of the Lord," or who else "has become His counsellor?"[112]

---

[111] Irenaeus of Lyons, "Irenæus against Heresies," in *The Apostolic Fathers with Justin Martyr and Irenaeus*, ed. Alexander Roberts, James Donaldson, and A. Cleveland Coxe, vol. 1, The Ante-Nicene Fathers (Buffalo, NY: Christian Literature Company, 1885), 521–522.

[112] Irenaeus of Lyons, "Irenæus against Heresies," in *The Apostolic Fathers with Justin Martyr and Irenaeus*, ed.

> "Since the Lord thus has redeemed us through His own blood, giving His soul for our souls, and His flesh for our flesh, and has also poured out the Spirit of the Father for the union and communion of God and man, imparting indeed God to men by means of the Spirit, and, on the other hand, attaching man to God by His own incarnation, and bestowing upon us at His coming immortality durably and truly, by means of communion with God,—all the doctrines of the heretics fall to ruin.[113]

Notice that Irenaeus declares the Word to be Jesus, the Son of God, both human and Divine. He also declares God to be imparted to us in the person of the Spirit. This is most certainly a confession of the Trinitarian faith.

Alexander Roberts, James Donaldson, and A. Cleveland Coxe, vol. 1, The Ante-Nicene Fathers (Buffalo, NY: Christian Literature Company, 1885), 526.

[113] Irenaeus of Lyons, "Irenæus against Heresies," in *The Apostolic Fathers with Justin Martyr and Irenaeus*, ed. Alexander Roberts, James Donaldson, and A. Cleveland Coxe, vol. 1, The Ante-Nicene Fathers (Buffalo, NY: Christian Literature Company, 1885), 527.

- "But He, the very same who formed Adam at the beginning, with whom also the Father spake, [saying], "Let Us make man after Our image and likeness," revealing Himself in these last times to men, formed visual organs (*visionem*) for him who had been blind [in that body which he had derived] from Adam. Wherefore also the Scripture, pointing out what should come to pass, says, that when Adam had hid himself because of his disobedience, the Lord came to him at eventide, called him forth, and said, "Where art thou?" That means that in the last times the very same Word of God came to call man, reminding him of his doings, living in which he had been hidden from the Lord. For just as at that time God spake to Adam at eventide, searching him out; so in the last times, by means of the same voice, searching out his posterity, He has visited them.[114]"

---

[114] Irenaeus of Lyons, "Irenæus against Heresies," in *The Apostolic Fathers with Justin Martyr and Irenaeus*, ed. Alexander Roberts, James Donaldson, and A. Cleveland Coxe, vol. 1, The Ante-Nicene Fathers (Buffalo, NY: Christian Literature Company, 1885), 543–544.

Irenaeus said it was with the Son whom the Father spoke when He said, "Let us…etc." This demonstrates Irenaeus' belief in the distinct Divine Persons of the Father and the Son.

- "The Father is indeed above all, and He is the Head of Christ; but the Word is through all things, and is Himself the Head of the Church; while the Spirit is in us all, and He is the living water, which the Lord grants to those who rightly believe in Him, and love Him, and who know that "there is one Father, who is above all, and through all, and in us all." And to these things does John also, the disciple of the Lord, bear witness, when he speaks thus in the Gospel: "In the beginning was the Word, and the Word was with God, and the Word was God. This was in the beginning with God. All things were made by Him, and without Him was nothing made."[6] And then he said of the Word Himself: "He was in the world, and the world was made by Him, and the world knew Him not. To His own things He came, and His own people received Him not. However, as many as did receive Him, to these gave He power to become the sons of

> God, to those that believe in His name." And again, showing the dispensation with regard to His human nature, John said: "And the Word was made flesh, and dwelt among us."[8] And in continuation he says, "And we beheld His glory, the glory as of the Only-begotten by the Father, full of grace and truth." He thus plainly points out to those willing to hear, that is, to those having ears, that there is one God, the Father over all, and one Word of God, who is through all, by whom all things have been made; and that this world belongs to Him, and was made by Him, according to the Father's will, and not by angels; nor by apostasy, defect, and ignorance; nor by any power of Prunicus, whom certain of them also call "the Mother;" nor by any other maker of the world ignorant of the Father.[115]"

Here Irenaeus shows his faith in the Godhood of the Word, who is Christ, and His distinction from the Father while declaring His faith in one God. Notice how

---

[115] Irenaeus of Lyons, "Irenæus against Heresies," in *The Apostolic Fathers with Justin Martyr and Irenaeus*, ed. Alexander Roberts, James Donaldson, and A. Cleveland Coxe, vol. 1, The Ante-Nicene Fathers (Buffalo, NY: Christian Literature Company, 1885), 546.

he says, "One God, the Father of all, and one Word of God…" He believed both to be God while also believing they were distinct persons.

- "But the Word of God is the superior above all, He who is loudly proclaimed in the law: "Hear, O Israel, the LORD thy God is one God;" and, "Thou shalt love the LORD thy God with all thy heart;" and, "Him shall thou adore, and Him alone shall thou serve." Then in the Gospel, casting down the apostasy by means of these expressions, He did both overcome the strong man by His Father's voice, and He acknowledges the commandment of the law to express His own sentiments, when He says, "Thou shall not tempt the LORD thy God." For He did not confound the adversary by the saying of any other, but by that belonging to His own Father, and thus overcame the strong man.[116]"

---

[116] Irenaeus of Lyons, "Irenæus against Heresies," in *The Apostolic Fathers with Justin Martyr and Irenaeus*, ed. Alexander Roberts, James Donaldson, and A. Cleveland Coxe, vol. 1, The Ante-Nicene Fathers (Buffalo, NY: Christian Literature Company, 1885), 550.

It would be difficult to conceive of a stronger affirmation of the existence of only one God while also holding the faith in the personal distinction between the Father and the Son, though both are the One God.

- "Christ, who was called the Son of God before the ages, was manifested in the fulness of time, in order that He might cleanse us through His blood, who were under the power of sin, presenting us as pure sons to His Father, if we yield ourselves obediently to the chastisement of the Spirit. And in the end of time He shall come to do away with all evil, and to reconcile all things, in order that there may be an end of all impurities.[117]"

The essential deity and eternity of the Son as well as His personal distinction from Father is herein taught.

---

[117] Irenaeus of Lyons, "Fragments from the Lost Writings of Irenæus," in *The Apostolic Fathers with Justin Martyr and Irenaeus*, ed. Alexander Roberts, James Donaldson, and A. Cleveland Coxe, vol. 1, The Ante-Nicene Fathers (Buffalo, NY: Christian Literature Company, 1885), 575.

- "In like manner also the three days which were before the luminaries, are types of the Trinity,[2] of God, and His Word, and His wisdom.[118]" [A.D. 115–168–181.] (Editor's Note: "Τριάδος. [The earliest use of this word "Trinity." It seems to have been used by this writer in his lost works, also; and, as a learned friends suggests, the use he makes of it is familiar. He does not lug it in as something novel: "types of the Trinity," he says, illustrating an accepted word, not introducing a new one.]"[119])

Need anything be said about this obvious statement? Yet we shall consider it, though we belabor

---

[118] Theophilus of Antioch, "Theophilus to Autolycus," in *Fathers of the Second Century: Hermas, Tatian, Athenagoras, Theophilus, and Clement of Alexandria (Entire)*, ed. Alexander Roberts, James Donaldson, and A. Cleveland Coxe, trans. Marcus Dods, vol. 2, The Ante-Nicene Fathers (Buffalo, NY: Christian Literature Company, 1885), 100–101.

[119] Alexander Roberts, James Donaldson, and A. Cleveland Coxe, eds., *Fathers of the Second Century: Hermas, Tatian, Athenagoras, Theophilus, and Clement of Alexandria (Entire)*, vol. 2, The Ante-Nicene Fathers (Buffalo, NY: Christian Literature Company, 1885).

the issue. The first pope dates to AD440 (Leo) thus, this cannot be a term that originated in the Roman Catholic religious system, which cannot exist without a pope. Furthermore, this statement precedes even the Council of Nicaea by more than a century.

- "That we are not atheists, therefore, seeing that we acknowledge one God, uncreated, eternal, invisible, impassible, incomprehensible, illimitable, who is apprehended by the understanding only and the reason, who is encompassed by light, and beauty, and spirit, and power ineffable, by whom the universe has been created through His Logos, and set in order, and is kept in being—I have sufficiently demonstrated. [I say "His Logos"], for we acknowledge also a Son of God. Nor let any one think it ridiculous that God should have a Son. For though the poets, in their fictions, represent the gods as no better than men, our mode of thinking is not the same as theirs, concerning either God the Father or the Son. But the Son of God is the Logos of the Father, in idea and in operation; for after the pattern of Him and by Him were all things made, the Father and the Son being one. And, the Son being in the Father and the Father in the Son, in oneness and power of spirit, the understanding and reason (νοῦς καὶ λόγος) of the Father is the Son of God. But if, in your surpassing intelligence, it occurs to you to inquire what is meant by the Son, I will state briefly that He is the first product of the Father, not as having been brought into existence (for from the beginning, God, who is the eternal mind [νοῦς], had the Logos in Himself, being from eternity instinct with Logos [λογικός]; but inasmuch as He came forth to be the idea and energizing power of all material things, which lay like a nature without attributes, and an inactive earth, the grosser particles being mixed up with the lighter. The prophetic Spirit also agrees with our statements. "The Lord," it says, "made me, the beginning of His ways to His works." The Holy Spirit Himself also, which operates in the prophets, we assert to be an effluence of God, flowing from Him, and returning back again like a beam of the sun. Who, then, would not be astonished to hear men who speak of God the Father, and of God the Son, and of the Holy Spirit, and who

> declare both their power in union and their distinction in order, called atheists? Nor is our teaching in what relates to the divine nature confined to these points; but we recognise also a multitude of angels and ministers,[11] whom God the Maker and Framer of the world distributed and appointed to their several posts by His Logos, to occupy themselves about the elements, and the heavens, and the world, and the things in it, and the goodly ordering of them all.[120]" [A.D. 177.]

The Trinitarian faith is plainly expressed here as being One God in three Persons or a Tri-Unity/Trinity. Notice also the confession of the eternal existence and Sonship of Christ as well as the insinuation of the Deity of the Spirit.

---

[120] Athenagoras, "A Plea for the Christians," in *Fathers of the Second Century: Hermas, Tatian, Athenagoras, Theophilus, and Clement of Alexandria (Entire)*, ed. Alexander Roberts, James Donaldson, and A. Cleveland Coxe, trans. B. P. Pratten, vol. 2, The Ante-Nicene Fathers (Buffalo, NY: Christian Literature Company, 1885), 133–134.

- "they know God and His Logos, what is the oneness of the Son with the Father, what the communion of the Father with the Son, what is the Spirit, what is the unity of these three, the Spirit, the Son, the Father, and their distinction in unity[121]"

This is explicitly Trinitarian. Again, note that Athenagorus wrote circa AD 177, almost one hundred-fifty years before the Nicene Council.

- "This Word, then, the Christ, the cause of both our being at first (for He was in God) and of our well-being, this very Word has now appeared as man, He alone being both, both God and man—the Author of all blessings to us; by whom we, being taught to live well, are sent on our way to life eternal. For, according to that inspired apostle of the Lord, "the grace of God

---

[121] Athenagoras, "A Plea for the Christians," in *Fathers of the Second Century: Hermas, Tatian, Athenagoras, Theophilus, and Clement of Alexandria (Entire)*, ed. Alexander Roberts, James Donaldson, and A. Cleveland Coxe, trans. B. P. Pratten, vol. 2, The Ante-Nicene Fathers (Buffalo, NY: Christian Literature Company, 1885), 134.

which bringeth salvation hath appeared to all men, teaching us, that, denying ungodliness and worldly lusts, we should live soberly, righteously, and godly, in this present world; looking for the blessed hope, and appearing of the glory of the great God and our Saviour Jesus Christ."[122]" [A.D. 153–193–217.]

Clement of Alexandria, though one who would not be as orthodox as earlier writers, was clearly Trinitarian, and that long before Roman Catholicism.

- "What the Holy Spirit says by Hosea, I will not shrink from quoting: "Lo, I am He that appointeth the thunder, and createth spirit; and His hands have established the host of heaven." And once more by Isaiah. And this utterance I will repeat: "I am," he says, "I am the LORD; I who speak righteousness, announce truth. Gather

---

[122] Clement of Alexandria, "Exhortation to the Heathen," in *Fathers of the Second Century: Hermas, Tatian, Athenagoras, Theophilus, and Clement of Alexandria (Entire)*, ed. Alexander Roberts, James Donaldson, and A. Cleveland Coxe, vol. 2, The Ante-Nicene Fathers (Buffalo, NY: Christian Literature Company, 1885), 173.

yourselves together, and come. Take counsel together, ye that are saved from the nations.[123]"

An expression of faith in the Deity of the Holy Spirit because what the Spirit says is, "I am the LORD." This being so, at this point in our study, we can safely conclude that Clement was Trinitarian.

- "The Spirit calls the Lord Himself a child, thus prophesying by Esaias: "Lo, to us a child has been born, to us a son has been given, on whose own shoulder the government shall be; and His name has been called the Angel of great Counsel." Who, then, is this infant child? He according to whose image we are made little children. By the same prophet is declared His greatness: "Wonderful, Counsellor, Mighty God, Everlasting Father, Prince of Peace; that He might fulfil His discipline: and of His peace there

---

[123] Clement of Alexandria, "Exhortation to the Heathen," in *Fathers of the Second Century: Hermas, Tatian, Athenagoras, Theophilus, and Clement of Alexandria (Entire)*, ed. Alexander Roberts, James Donaldson, and A. Cleveland Coxe, vol. 2, The Ante-Nicene Fathers (Buffalo, NY: Christian Literature Company, 1885), 194.

> shall be no end." O the great God! O the perfect child! The Son in the Father, and the Father in the Son. And how shall not the discipline of this child be perfect, which extends to all, leading as a schoolmaster us as children who are His little ones? He has stretched forth to us those hands of His that are conspicuously worthy of trust. To this child additional testimony is borne by John, "the greatest prophet among those born of women:" Behold the Lamb of God!" For since Scripture calls the infant children lambs, it has also called Him—God the Word—who became man for our sakes, and who wished in all points to be made like to us"—"the Lamb of God"—Him, namely, that is the Son of God, the child of the Father.[124]"

Once again, we find the essential Deity of the Son as well as His personal distinction presented. Clement shows his faith in the essential unity between

---

124 Clement of Alexandria, "The Instructor," in *Fathers of the Second Century: Hermas, Tatian, Athenagoras, Theophilus, and Clement of Alexandria (Entire)*, ed. Alexander Roberts, James Donaldson, and A. Cleveland Coxe, vol. 2, The Ante-Nicene Fathers (Buffalo, NY: Christian Literature Company, 1885), 215.

Father and Son as well as the personal distinction between them.

- "So that it is veritably clear that the God of all is only one good, just Creator, and the Son in the Father, to whom be glory for ever and ever, Amen. [125]"

Notice the essential union of the Son and the Father as well as the personal distinction between them.

- "Be gracious, O Instructor, to us Thy children, Father, Charioteer of Israel, Son and Father, both in One, O Lord. Grant to us who obey Thy precepts, that we may perfect the likeness of the image, and with all our power know Him who is the good God and not a harsh judge. And do Thou Thyself cause that all of us who have our conversation in Thy peace, who have

---

[125] Clement of Alexandria, "The Instructor," in *Fathers of the Second Century: Hermas, Tatian, Athenagoras, Theophilus, and Clement of Alexandria (Entire)*, ed. Alexander Roberts, James Donaldson, and A. Cleveland Coxe, vol. 2, The Ante-Nicene Fathers (Buffalo, NY: Christian Literature Company, 1885), 228.

been translated into Thy commonwealth, having sailed tranquilly over the billows of sin, may be wafted in calm by Thy Holy Spirit, by the ineffable wisdom, by night and day to the perfect day; and giving thanks may praise, and praising thank the Alone Father and Son, Son and Father, the Son, Instructor and Teacher, with the Holy Spirit, all in One, in whom is all, for whom all is One, for whom is eternity, whose members we all are, whose glory the æons are; for the All-good, All-lovely, All-wise, All-just One. To whom be glory both now and for ever. Amen.[126]"

Here we again see a confession of the unity of the three persons of the One True God.

- "OF the Gnostic so much has been cursorily, as it were, written. We

---

[126] Clement of Alexandria, "The Instructor," in *Fathers of the Second Century: Hermas, Tatian, Athenagoras, Theophilus, and Clement of Alexandria (Entire)*, ed. Alexander Roberts, James Donaldson, and A. Cleveland Coxe, vol. 2, The Ante-Nicene Fathers (Buffalo, NY: Christian Literature Company, 1885), 295.

proceed now to the sequel, and must again contemplate faith; for there are some that draw the distinction, that faith has reference to the Son, and knowledge to the Spirit. But it has escaped their notice that, in order to believe truly in the Son, we must believe that He is the Son, and that He came, and how, and for what, and respecting His passion; and we must know who is the Son of God. Now neither is knowledge without faith, nor faith without knowledge. Nor is the Father without the Son; for the Son is with the Father. And the Son is the true teacher respecting the Father; and that we may believe in the Son, we must know the Father, with whom also is the Son. Again, in order that we may know the Father, we must believe in the Son, that it is the Son of God who teaches; for from faith to knowledge by the Son is the Father. And the knowledge of the Son and Father, which is according to the gnostic rule—that which in reality is gnostic—is the attainment and comprehension of the truth by the truth.[127]"

---

[127] Clement of Alexandria, "The Stromata, or Miscellanies," in *Fathers of the Second Century:*

The writer once again presents the essential unity of the Father and Son as well as their distinctive persons. He also gives passing notice to the Spirit.

- "And it is the name of God that is expressed; since, as the Son sees the goodness of the Father, God the Saviour works, being called the first principle of all things, which was imaged forth from the invisible God first, and before the ages, and which fashioned all things which came into being after itself. [128]"

Though the Son is called God, yet He is quite obviously personally distinguished from the Father, as

---

Hermas, Tatian, Athenagoras, Theophilus, and Clement of Alexandria (Entire), ed. Alexander Roberts, James Donaldson, and A. Cleveland Coxe, vol. 2, The Ante-Nicene Fathers (Buffalo, NY: Christian Literature Company, 1885), 444.

[128] Clement of Alexandria, "The Stromata, or Miscellanies," in *Fathers of the Second Century: Hermas, Tatian, Athenagoras, Theophilus, and Clement of Alexandria (Entire)*, ed. Alexander Roberts, James Donaldson, and A. Cleveland Coxe, vol. 2, The Ante-Nicene Fathers (Buffalo, NY: Christian Literature Company, 1885), 453.

He declares the Father to men. Clement also confesses his faith in the eternal nature of the Son as God yet distinct in person from the Father.

- "the Son, which ever glorifies the Father[129]"

Need a comment be made?

- "God, then, being not a subject for demonstration, cannot be the object of science. But the Son is wisdom, and knowledge, and truth, and all else that has affinity thereto. He is also susceptible of demonstration and of description. And all the powers of the Spirit, becoming collectively one thing, terminate in the same point—that is, in the Son. But He is incapable of being declared, in respect of the idea of each one of His powers. And

---

[129] Clement of Alexandria, "The Stromata, or Miscellanies," in *Fathers of the Second Century: Hermas, Tatian, Athenagoras, Theophilus, and Clement of Alexandria (Entire)*, ed. Alexander Roberts, James Donaldson, and A. Cleveland Coxe, vol. 2, The Ante-Nicene Fathers (Buffalo, NY: Christian Literature Company, 1885), 376.

> the Son is neither simply one thing as one thing, nor many things as parts, but one thing as all things; whence also He is all things. For He is the circle of all powers rolled and united into one unity. Wherefore the Word is called the Alpha and the Omega, of whom alone the end becomes beginning, and ends again at the original beginning without any break. Wherefore also to believe in Him, and by Him, is to become a unit, being indissolubly united in Him; and to disbelieve is to be separated, disjoined, divided.[130]"

As complicated or confusing as this quote seems to be, the basic reality is the writer believed in the essential Deity of each Person of the Godhead, Father, Son, and Holy Spirit, all being One God in Three Persons.

---

130 Clement of Alexandria, "The Stromata, or Miscellanies," in *Fathers of the Second Century: Hermas, Tatian, Athenagoras, Theophilus, and Clement of Alexandria (Entire)*, ed. Alexander Roberts, James Donaldson, and A. Cleveland Coxe, vol. 2, The Ante-Nicene Fathers (Buffalo, NY: Christian Literature Company, 1885), 438.

- “I understand nothing else than the Holy Trinity to be meant; for the third is the Holy Spirit, and the Son is the second, by whom all things were made according to the will of the Father.[131]”

Clement, in the late second or early third century, proclaimed the Trinitarian faith and used the word, “Trinity,” long before the Nicaean Council and long before Roman Catholicism was established.

- “What therefore he says, “from the beginning,” the Presbyter explained to this effect, that the beginning of generation is not separated from the beginning of the Creator. For when he says, “That which was from the beginning,” he touches upon the generation without beginning of the Son, who is co-existent with the Father. There was, then, a Word

---

[131] Clement of Alexandria, “The Stromata, or Miscellanies,” in *Fathers of the Second Century: Hermas, Tatian, Athenagoras, Theophilus, and Clement of Alexandria (Entire)*, ed. Alexander Roberts, James Donaldson, and A. Cleveland Coxe, vol. 2, The Ante-Nicene Fathers (Buffalo, NY: Christian Literature Company, 1885), 468.

> importing an unbeginning eternity; as also the Word itself, that is, the Son of God, who being, by equality of substance, one with the Father, is eternal and uncreate. That He was always the Word, is signified by saying, "In the beginning was the Word." But by the expression, "we have seen with our eyes," he signifies the Lord's presence in the flesh, "and our hands have handled," he says, "of the Word of life."[132]"

The con-substantiality (being of the same substance) of the Son with the Father is explicitly stated here while also affirming the Father and Son as distinct Persons. In other words, the writer believed the Son and the Father, though distinct persons, are one being.

- """"The life was manifested." For in the Gospel he thus speaks: "And what

---

[132] Clement of Alexandria, "Fragments of Clemens Alexandrinus," in *Fathers of the Second Century: Hermas, Tatian, Athenagoras, Theophilus, and Clement of Alexandria (Entire)*, ed. Alexander Roberts, James Donaldson, and A. Cleveland Coxe, trans. William Wilson, vol. 2, The Ante-Nicene Fathers (Buffalo, NY: Christian Literature Company, 1885), 574.

> was made, in Him was life, and the life was the light of men."
> "And we show unto you that eternal life, which was with the Father, and was manifested unto you."
>
> He signifies by the appellation of Father, that the Son also existed always, without beginning.[133]

Notice the faith in the eternal Sonship of Christ, which is a declaration both of His Deity and His distinct personhood.

- "But to him who directs his eye to salvation and desires it, and asks with boldness and vehemence for its bestowal, the good Father who is in heaven will give the true purification and the changeless life. To whom, by His Son Jesus Christ, the Lord of the living and dead, and by the Holy

---

[133] Clement of Alexandria, "Fragments of Clemens Alexandrinus," in *Fathers of the Second Century: Hermas, Tatian, Athenagoras, Theophilus, and Clement of Alexandria (Entire)*, ed. Alexander Roberts, James Donaldson, and A. Cleveland Coxe, trans. William Wilson, vol. 2, The Ante-Nicene Fathers (Buffalo, NY: Christian Literature Company, 1885), 574.

> Spirit, be glory, honour, power,
> eternal majesty, both now and ever,
> from generation to generation, and
> from eternity to eternity. Amen.[134]"

Can there be a statement which is much more explicitly Trinitarian than this?

Concluding Comments

The above quotes are confined to a specific group of writers who were associated with Eastern Christianity and not Latin Christianity, since Roman Catholicism has its origins in Latin Christianity and this writer did not wish to open himself to the accusation of quoting Roman Catholic writers. The writers quoted also were either geographically or chronologically closely related to the apostles. Papias, Polycarp, and Irenaeus were also personally related to the apostles and able to tell us what the apostles believed and preached.

---

[134] Clement of Alexandria, "Who Is the Rich Man That Shall Be Saved?," in *Fathers of the Second Century: Hermas, Tatian, Athenagoras, Theophilus, and Clement of Alexandria (Entire)*, ed. Alexander Roberts, James Donaldson, and A. Cleveland Coxe, trans. William Wilson, vol. 2, The Ante-Nicene Fathers (Buffalo, NY: Christian Literature Company, 1885), 604.

Having examined a multitude of quotations and having left out quite a few, it is this writer's settled conclusion that history refutes the assertion that the Trinity is a Roman Catholic invention, and is instead Biblical, apostolic, and predates Roman Catholicism by so much time that there can be no historical possibility of the origin of Trinitarian teaching being Roman Catholic.

Appendix

Oneness Pentecostalism

The Pentecostal movement in the United States of America had its beginning in 1906, during a revival meeting in Los Angeles. This meeting was called "The Azusa Street Revival." The preacher for this revival was William Seymour, a one-eyed black man from Houston, TX, who was a disciple of Charles Parham, a then well-known preacher in the fledgling Pentecostal movement. This movement was seemingly an attempt to replicate the Welsh Revival.[135] The message preached was that speaking in tongues is the first evidence of the baptism in the Holy Spirit.

From its beginning during the Azusa Street Revival, Pentecostalism has had many women preachers and pastors contrary to the Scriptural command for women to be submissive to their husbands, keeping silence and learning in silence, as well as contrary to the prohibition of women preaching. One Julia Hutchins had a church in Los Angeles, and she lent her church and influence to this so-called revival.[136]

As people began to speak in their version of tongues, news spread and the meetings and number of those purportedly speaking in tongues grew. These

---

135

https://www.apostolicarchives.com/articles/article/8801925/173190.htm (Accessed May 09, 2025)

136 Ibid

meetings eventually were moved to a building in a black ghetto on Azusa Street, and they named it "The Apostolic Faith Mission." Soon there were hundreds in attendance.[137]

Initial responses among the general public were not kind. Even Charles Parham is reported to have called some of the occurrences in their meetings, "freak imitation of Pentecost."[138] "Among first-hand accounts were reports of the blind having their sight restored, diseases cured instantly, and immigrants speaking in German, Yiddish, and Spanish all being spoken to in their native language by uneducated black members, who translated the languages into English by "supernatural ability". Singing was sporadic and in *a cappella* or occasionally in tongues. There were periods of extended silence. Attenders were occasionally slain in the Spirit. Visitors gave their testimony, and members read aloud testimonies that were sent to the mission by mail. There was prayer for the gift of tongues. There was prayer in tongues for the sick, for missionaries, and whatever requests were given by attenders or mailed in. There was spontaneous preaching and altar calls for salvation, sanctification and baptism of the Holy Spirit. Lawrence Catley, whose family attended the revival, said that in most services preaching consisted of Seymour opening a Bible and worshippers coming forward to preach or testify as they were led by the Holy

---

137 Ibid

138 Ibid

Spirit. Many people would continually shout throughout the meetings. The members of the mission never took an offering, but there was a receptacle near the door for anyone that wanted to support the revival. The core membership of the Azusa Street Mission was never much more than 50–60 individuals with hundreds and thousands of people visiting or staying temporarily over the years.[139]"

From this point forward, the Pentecostal movement grew both in the United States and abroad. Seymour began publishing a newspaper, "The Apostolic Faith," which soon had a circulation of twenty thousand. "Today millions of Pentecostals and Charismatics trace their beginnings to Azusa Street…"[140]

Organizations

It would be difficult to trace and describe all the organizations that adhere to Oneness Pentecostal doctrines. There are many independent congregations who declare they are only under the headship of Christ and give no allegiance at all to any organization. There are two large organizations which profess the so-called

---

139 https://www.apostolicarchives.com/articles/article/8801925/173190.htm (Accessed May 9, 2025)

140 https://revival-library.org/histories/1906-azusa-street-revival/ (Accessed May 9, 2025)

Apostolic or Oneness Pentecostal faith: "The United Pentecostal Church International[141]" and "The Apostolic Church of Jesus Christ.[142]"

It is interesting to note that the ACJC has roots in Houston, TX as did the William Seymour. In fact, they are explicit in linking themselves to Azusa Street.[143] The UPCI also traces their roots in the Azusa Street Revival.

Beliefs

1. The absolute Oneness of God. Oneness Pentecostals are not Trinitarians but are adamantly opposed to the doctrine of the Trinity.

   "There is one God, who has revealed Himself as Father; through His Son, in redemption; and as

---

141 https://upci.org/about-the-upci/ (Accessed May 9, 2025)

142 https://www.acjcii.org/history (Accessed May 9, 2025)

143

https://www.acjcii.org/_files/ugd/25c9f2_d8ab576449c344a381617f5e0f9bfae3.pdf (Accessed May 9, 2025)

the Holy Spirit, by emanation. Jesus Christ is God manifested in flesh. He is both God and man. (See Deuteronomy 6:4; Ephesians 4:4-6; Colossians 2:9; I Timothy 3:16.)[144]"

"The beautiful message of Scripture is that our Creator became our Savior. The God against whom we sinned is the One who forgives us. God loved us so much that He came in flesh to save us. He gave of Himself; He did not send someone else. Moreover, our Creator-Savior is also the indwelling Spirit who is ever-present to help us. God told us how to live and then came to live among us. He showed us how to live in the flesh and laid down His human life to purchase our salvation. Now He abides within us and enables us to live according to His will. Jesus Christ is the one God incarnate, and in Him we have everything we need: healing, deliverance, victory, and salvation (Colossians 2:9-10). By recognizing the almighty God in Jesus Christ, we restore correct biblical belief and experience apostolic power.[145]"

"Uncompromising monotheism is one of the clearest themes of Scripture. Simply stated, God is absolutely and indivisibly one. "Hear, O Israel:

---

144 https://upci.org/our-beliefs/ (Accessed May 9, 2025)

145 ibid

The Lord our God is one Lord" (Deuteronomy 6:4). There are no essential distinctions in His eternal nature. All names and titles of the Deity—such as God (Elohim), Jehovah (Yahweh), Lord, Father, Word, and Holy Spirit—refer to one and the same being. Any plurality associated with God merely relates to attributes, titles, roles, manifestations, or aspects of God's self-revelation to humans.[146]"

2. Baptism is necessary to salvation.

   "There is only one way to become a member of the Church of Jesus Christ: "Ye must be born again of water and of the Spirit" (John 3:5). "Repent and be baptized, every one of you in the name of Jesus Christ, for the remission of sins," as in Acts 2:38, "and ye shall receive the gift of the Holy Ghost," with the signs following as in Acts 2:4. We enter into the Body of Christ, the true Church, by baptism or birth of water and Spirit. "For by one Spirit are we all baptized into

---

[146] https://upci.org/wp-content/uploads/2022/09/The_True_Humanity_of_Jesus_Christ.pdf (Accessed May 9, 2025)

one body" (1 Corinthians 12:13). See also 1 Corinthians 12:27-28, John 3:5-8.[147]

"The saving gospel is the good news that Jesus died for our sins, was buried, and rose again. We obey the gospel (II Thessalonians 1:8; I Peter 4:17) by repentance (death to sin), water baptism in the name of Jesus Christ (burial), and the baptism of the Holy Spirit with the initial sign of speaking in tongues as the Spirit gives the utterance (resurrection). (See I Corinthians 15:1-4; Acts 2:4, 37-39; Romans 6:3-4.)[148]"

"the application of grace and the expression of faith come as a person obeys Acts 2:38, thereby receiving the new birth promised by Jesus.[149]"

"This new creation is accomplished by the new birth of water and the Spirit as described in John

---

147 https://www.acjcii.org/_files/ugd/25c9f2_d8ab576449c344a381617f5e0f9bfae3.pdf (Accessed May 9, 2025)

148 https://upci.org/our-beliefs/ (Accessed May 9, 2025)

149 https://upci.org/oneness-pentecostalism/ (Accessed May 9, 2025)

3:5-6: “Jesus answered, Verily, verily, I say unto thee, Except a man be born of water and of the Spirit, he cannot enter into the kingdom of God. That which is born of the flesh is flesh; and that which is born of the Spirit is spirit.” Thus in the New Testament, man’s holiness is God’s character inborn into his or her nature by the infilling presence of the Spirit of God. The birth of the Spirit makes a person a new creature.[150]”

“To be saved by water baptism, it must be administered by burial in water, in the name of the Lord Jesus Christ, for there is no other name given among men whereby we must be saved. The life of the blood of Jesus Christ is connected with water baptism when it is administered in His name.[151]”

---

150 https://upci.org/wp-content/uploads/2022/10/Holiness.pdf (Accessed May 9, 2025)

151 https://www.acjcii.org/_files/ugd/25c9f2_d8ab576449c344a381617f5e0f9bfae3.pdf (Accessed May 9, 2025)

3. The possibility of a believer losing his salvation.

"And the Lord said unto Moses, whosoever hath sinned against me, him I will blot out of my book" (Exodus 32:33). In Revelation 3:5 it is written, "He that overcometh … I will not blot out his name out of the book of life.[152]"

"One must be thoroughly saved from sin, wholly sanctified, and filled with the Holy Ghost to escape the judgments of God and to have the hope of enjoying the glory of eternal life.[153]"

"Issues of holiness are not salvation issues in and of themselves; rather, they are Christian maturity ("sanctification") issues. "Follow peace with all men, and holiness, without which no man shall see the Lord." (Hebrews 12:14) However, if we choose not to obey God in these areas, our willful disobedience will eventually become a salvation

---

152 https://www.acjcii.org/_files/ugd/25c9f2_d8ab576449c344a381617f5e0f9bfae3.pdf (Accessed May 9, 2025)

153 ibid

issue. (1 Corinthians 3:16-17, 2 Corinthians 6:17 - 7:1)"[154]

4. Speaking in tongues is the evidence of salvation.

   "Speaking in tongues as the Spirit gives utterance is the initial evidence of the baptism of the Holy Ghost (Acts 2:4-19, 9:17-18 with 1 Corinthians 14:18, Acts 10:44, 19:6).[155]"

   "Why did God choose speaking in tongues as a sign? We cannot be absolutely sure, but we must accept His plan by faith.[156]"

---

[154] https://globaltracts.com/wp-content/uploads/2019/01/ENG-LIFEClass_Salvation101Adapted.pdf (Accessed May 9, 2025)

[155] https://www.acjcii.org/_files/ugd/25c9f2_d8ab576449c344a381617f5e0f9bfae3.pdf (Accessed May 9, 2025)

[156] https://globaltracts.com/wp-content/uploads/2019/01/ENG-

Why Call Oneness Pentecostals A Cult?

The first mark of a cult seen in Oneness Pentecostals is their aberrant belief concerning the nature and person(s) of God. Instead of believing the Biblical doctrine of the Trinity, they are adamantly anti-Trinitarian, often declaring the Trinity to be a belief in three gods. This is very problematic because the god of Oneness Pentecostalism is not the same as the Triune God of Scripture; neither is their Jesus the Christ of the Scripture.

Then their doctrine of salvation is very much a works-based doctrine. It even demands works for one to remain saved, although they do not use those words. Instead, they declare one can lose his salvation by failing to be holy.

In many cases, Oneness Pentecostals are often led by a dynamic and authoritarian leader in the pulpit. Often the authority of such a pastor is nearly absolute, which is a characteristic of a cult.

We can also notice the way many Oneness Pentecostals withdraw from their friends and family members who disagree with them on these issues. There is often an "us against them" mentality which leads many to even withdraw or even fully separate from one's

---

LIFEClass_Salvation101Adapted.pdf (Accessed May 9, 2025)

closest family members. In my experience, some Oneness Pentecostals will openly declare their beliefs and openly pronounce as apostate or condemned all who have not been baptized in Jesus' Name and who have not spoken in tongues. This, too, is a mark of a cult.

Further reading:

Marks of A Cult:
https://thebaptistsentinel.com/2025/03/07/marks-of-a-cult-2/

Articles on The Trinity:
https://thebaptistsentinel.com/theology-proper-the-doctrine-of-god/

Made in the USA
Columbia, SC
13 June 2025

59392294R00124